the MONKLANDS

AN ILLUSTRATED ARCHITECTURAL ——— GUIDE ———

I AM DELIGHTED that the considerable architectural heritage of The Monklands is recognised in this excellent guide. Few parts of Scotland more vividly reveal the transformation from rural to industrial wrought by the Industrial Revolution. Airdrie, once a weavers' town, predates the dramatic changes but Coatbridge is the epitome of a period of dramatic industrial growth. Summerlee Heritage Park, one of Scotland's most fascinating museums, tells the astonishing history but the buildings too tell the story of the two towns, and the villages clustered round them, which constitute the modern Monklands District.

THE RT. HON. JOHN SMITH, QC MP

© Author: Allan Peden
Series editor: Charles McKean
Series consultant: David Walker
Cover design: Dorothy Steedman
Editorial consultant: Duncan McAra

Royal Incorporation of Architects in Scotland
ISBN 1873190 05 0
First published 1992

Cover illustrations: 'The Iron Burgh' by Walter MacAdam 'a Glasgow artist of some repute'. Presented by George Garrett, ironmaster, on 12th July 1900 to the Burgh, to be hung on the grand staircase of the new Municipal Buildings. Mr Garrett commented that 'it will show future generations of inhabitants what blast furnaces looked like — as they may not be much in evidence'. View towards Kirk o' Shotts (photo B Bickerton)

Typesetting, page make-up and picture scans: Almond Design, Edinburgh
Printed by Pillans & Wilson, Edinburgh

A

INTRODUCTION

Western Monklands consists of a gentle native landscape shaped by the glacial drift of the last Ice Age, which left a series of low clay knolls or drumlins on its plain, forming the seven hills of Coatbridge, later riven by the many small watercourses which flow into the North Calder Water. To the east, the ground rises gradually to the Slamannan plateau with Airdrie on its rim and the Moffat hills behind, forming a great tract of high and windswept open moorland, stretching out towards West Lothian and the Falkirk braes.

The earliest known human settlement in the Monklands was by small bands of Mesolithic hunter gatherers (*c*.6000 BC) whose primitive stone tools have been found in the deep peat moss beside **Woodend Loch**. There were Bronze Age settlements at **Annathill**, **Drumpellier** and near **Caldercruix**, and an Iron Age crannog – a group of dwellings built on timber stilts over an artificial island – in Lochend Loch was occupied from perhaps 100 BC until about the time the Scots colonised the area from the west around AD 500.

Although the Antonine Wall was constructed only a few miles to the north in AD 143, it does not appear that the Romans showed any interest in this primordial land and a further millennium had to pass before Cistercian monks were to settle here and farm the area, thus lending it their name.

Opposite *A Cistercian lay brother in working habit from* A Concise History of the Cistercian Order

Scottish Record Office

There is no mention of any buildings in these charters, indeed later commentators record the whole district as *uncultivated and devoted to flocks and beasts of the chase.*

Being a working order dedicated to the simple monastic precepts of St Benedict, the Cistercians established a sheep grange at Drumpellier, whose wool became highly prized and exported to the east. Thus were the origins of the King's Highway, a track which joined

The original Charter of 1162, *(left)* by which King Malcolm IV granted to the Monks of Newbattle Abbey land roughly covering the area now known as Monklands District, along with the Steward's Charter of 1323 by which Walter the Steward of Scotland gave the monks right of passage for trade through to their Lothian estates, formally referring to this area for the first time as the *Munklands*, can still be seen in the Scottish Record Office in Edinburgh.

The Ross map of the Monklands 1776

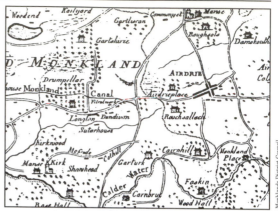

The Ross map of the Monklands 1776

Monklands District Council

Edinburgh to Glasgow from the late 12th century, passing through what was later to become Airdrie and over the Cottbrig, where Coatbridge was eventually to develop. Having established the track, the monks used their Caledonian Forest oaks to build massive wagons for this trade and characteristically also created a business in manufacturing these.

A corn mill was built *c.*1220 on the North Calder Water at Haggs to serve their extensive grain crops, and a chapel founded at Kipps in the mid 14th century, also to serve as a civil courthouse for the Barony Courts of the province (none of which has survived).

The Cistercians, who also worked the lead mines of Wanlockhead, became the first to discover the Monklands' open-cast coal deposits. In 1435 Aeneas Sylvius, later Pope Pius II, was amazed to see, on his visit to Scotland, *the poor, almost in a state of nakedness at church doors, depart with joy in their faces on receiving stones as alms* (the Italian was unfamiliar with coal).

The Reformation abruptly ended the Cistercians' benign influence, and until the 18th century the Monklands figures merely as land to be negotiated on the route between Kentigern's city and the Capital.

It must have seemed that history had relegated the Monklands to the status of some sparsely populated and bucolic footnote. But the *black stanes* and the singular geology of the area determined otherwise. This footnote suddenly burst into dramatic headlines as the Monklands was transformed from a pastoral landscape into the iron crucible of the Industrial Revolution. The New Scotland came to be forged here.

How to use the Guide: The volume is a guide to an area to which, only a decade ago, few might have been drawn to in search of cultural evidence. But here, in the Monklands, is the history of rural, industrial and post-industrial Scotland and a new Lowland society, forged by the ironmasters, then left abused and abandoned by the onward course of developing technology.

Thus the architecture of the district charts its social history in a direct way, as cottages gave way to miners' rows, and later as the giant empty sheds of failed heavy industry became history. Here is a glimpse of the rich social history of the area, and the attitudes and cultural concerns of its society.

Sequence: The Guide begins in Airdrie, the more venerable of the two main settlements and then into the surrounding villages: Glenmavis (at the time of the disjunction of the Parishes of Old and New Monkland in 1655 a larger centre of population than Airdrie itself), the mining communities of Plains and Longriggend, the paper town of Caldercruix and memories of coal and iron stone at Salsburgh.

To the east: Kirk o' Shotts, then the twin industrial villages of Chapelhall and Calderbank. Coatbridge comes next (as in history), then the coal village of Bargeddie, and Glenboig, once the centre of the Scots fireclay industry and little Annathill, vestige of a once great mining community.

Text Arrangement: Entries follow the format of name (or street number), address, date and architect. Descriptions of streets and lesser buildings have been contained within paragraphs. Illustrations have been included of buildings now demolished. The dates given are those of the completion of the buildings (if known) or design. The accompanying margin text deals with historical aspects of the Monklands.

Map References: Numbers on the town maps, which cover the area of the Guide, do not refer to page numbers, but to the reference numbers in the text. (The index refers to page numbers.)

Access to Properties: Some of the buildings are open to the public, or are visible from a public road or footpath. A few are private and readers are requested to respect occupiers' privacy.

Sponsors: This Guide would not have been possible without the support of Monklands District Council, whose generous financial assistance has lowered greatly its cover price.

AIRDRIE

When fairs cam roun', the Airdrie chiels
Each took his lassie tae the reels
Threw aff their coat an' made their heels
Crack in the air.
Ilk house resoundin' in the squeals
On Airdrie Fair

Airdrie Fair, J McHutchison, 1858

Early legend relates that the great Caledonian poet, Merlin, was present here at the Battle of Arderyth in AD 577, when the forces of Rydderech the Bountiful, King of Strathclyde, and patron of St Mungo, signally defeated Aidan the Perfidious, thus securing the independence of Strathclyde, and allowing St Mungo to pursue his work in Glasgow. Merlin was awarded a golden torc for his celebratory verses, despite appearing for the losing side.

Airdrie figures briefly in the Register of the Great Seal of 1373, but remained a rural hamlet until 1695 when the progressive laird Robert Hamilton secured an Act of Parliament granting a Burgh Charter which made Airdrie a market town by allowing a weekly market and four annual fairs. At that time, it was but a *clachan with a few hundred folk engaged in weaving, distilling, brewing and candle making*, surrounded by *dreary, barren lands in which part of the Old Caledonian Forest still remained*. The town developed as a handloom weaving centre, but until 1840 its buildings remained almost entirely single-storey thatched cottages. When a gentleman named Paton erected the first two-storey building in the High Street the villagers spoke of this extraordinary development as *Paton's Folly*.

For a time, Airdrie's lofty position on its plateau some 200 ft above neighbouring Coatbridge put it at a commercial disadvantage as the latter profited from the Monklands Canal and the iron foundries which were later to line its towpaths. Much of the vital ironstone, however, was to be found around Airdrie. As handloom weaving declined with the introduction of the power loom, weavers found employment in the ironstone and coal pits, joined by both a great influx of Irish immigrants after the potato famine of the mid 1840s and Highlanders dispossessed by the Clearances.

Industrial development brought Airdrie a similar fate to Coatbridge: *for a while industrial prosperity held sway and beneath its black smokey shadow the peaceful market town of Airdrie died and was re-born as a busy industrial centre, whose rapid growth left the problems of slums, overcrowding and public health*. This low point in the fortunes of the burgh prompted an incoming sheriff to declare: *I am now located in a town socially and atmospherically the most benighted in*

18th century thatched cottages in Airdrie (demolished)

McArthur

Airdrie Town Council in 1879

McArthur

Scotland. Such were the progeny of the Scotland of the 19th-century industrial revolution. Since then, Airdrie has been greatly resuscitated but much of the surrounding environment is still struggling to come to terms with the legacy of the decline and fall of its empire of heavy industry.

AIRDRIE : Central
Wellwynd
Wellwynd, which runs steeply down from the High Street to Stirling Street, was one of the most notoriously overcrowded of Airdrie's wynds, a mixture of terraced weavers' cottages interspersed with lodging houses to serve its foundry, forge and engine works. In 1842, the local clergy testified that some of the lodgings housed as many as fourteen persons per room. By comparison today Wellwynd is fragmented and incoherent.

To the Trustees of the late Jane Smith,
AIRDRIE IRON FOUNDRY.

Robert Hamilton, Covenanting Laird
(1650-1701)
The transformation of Airdrie from a 'fermtoun' to a planned village was initiated by Robert Hamilton, the radical Laird of Airdrie House. With his father, Sir William Hamilton of Preston, who was also a known reformer, he had fought for the Covenant at Drumclog, but was forced to flee to Holland after the rout at Bothwell Bridge, while Airdrie House was taken as a barracks for Claverhouse's dragoons. He returned to incarceration at Edinburgh tolbooth, being released in 1693 and devoted much of his remaining years to improvements at Airdrie. The 1695 Act of Parliament which Hamilton promoted, established the Airdrie Fairs and assisted the sale of the planned feus which he marketed in the village. When he succeeded to the estates and honours of the Prestons late in life he rather typically refused to adopt the title.

Left *Airdrie Iron Foundry, Wellwynd, 1870*

1 **Weavers' Cottages Museum**,
23-25 Wellwynd, *c.*1780 (*right*)
It is appropriate that the oldest surviving buildings in central Airdrie are a pair of weavers' cottages saved from dereliction by Monklands District Council and renovated by Harley & Murray in 1988-9. The upper of the cottages is a sanitised reconstruction of a but and ben weaver's house as it might have been *c.*1850, the lower an exhibition gallery. They exemplify the cottages whose thatched terraces lined every street in the town before 1800; **No 23** housed three families, totalling sixteen persons, in 1861.

2 **Wellwynd Church**, Wellwynd, 1847
On the raised site of the original church, Airdrie's first public building was erected in 1789. The quatrefoil balustrade and twin

Above *West Parish Church.*
Right *Wellwynd Church*

The Airdrie Weavers
Airdrie was from its earliest
days a centre of handloom
weaving. Cotton weaving for
the mass market soon
superseded linen and woollens
as the main product, the looms
almost exclusively being
worked by the menfolk. Their
families were often employed in
needlework, spinning and
winding the reels with some
hardy wives working as porters
to carry the finished materials
on foot to the Glasgow
manufacturers who contracted-
out the work, also collecting the
raw materials for the next
order. This was a hazardous 30-
mile round-trip over a track
frequented by robbers and
footpads. Airdrie weavers later
formed a number of renowned
friendly societies to provide
financial relief for any of their
members fallen on hard times.
*Then here's tae the Weavers, wi
a hip hip hurra
An' it werna for the Weavers,
what wad we dae
we'd hae empty pouches, an' be
bare backit tae
An' it werna for the Honourable
Weavers.*

The Honourable Weavers, a
song dedicated to the Airdrie
Weavers' Society (1781-1966)

finials of this simple Gothic frontage are
something of a local landmark.

3 **West Parish Church**, Wellwynd, 1834,
Alex Baird
An impressive classical frontage in grey
sandstone set back from the road for effect and
distinguished by giant Tuscan pilasters
supporting a raised pediment with a central
belltower and cupola, *Erected by friends of the
Church of Scotland.* The small porch at the
entrance was added by A McGregor Mitchell in
1890 when the interior was recast in Gothic.

5 **Airdrie Savings Bank**, Wellwynd, 1925,
J M Arthur
A sequence of great grey granite columns gives
this building the commanding presence
befitting a successful independent bank.
   Turning the corner into Stirling Street is
leaner 1920s classical in creamy Blaxter stone
from Northumberland upon a grey granite base
which complements the 19th-century frontages.
The entrance on the splay is surmounted
grandly by a bronze family group by Petrie of
Glasgow – apparently of an Airdrie mother
extolling the virtues of thrift to her brood.

Airdrie Savings Bank

4 Airdrie Library, Wellwynd, 1926,
J M Arthur
Comparable to the adjacent Savings Bank
which contributed to the cost of the sandstone
and granite and gifted the site. Twin Doric
columns give emphasis to the entrance. This
replaced the original library in Anderson Street
and was also largely funded by Dr Andrew
Carnegie. Still containing its original
observatory, the Library also shelters the
Covenanting standard of the East Monklands
originally carried by John Main, the laird of
Ballochney, at the Battle of Bothwell Brig in
1679.

Airdrie Library

Stirling Street
This main thoroughfare was formed in 1795
and replaced the old King's Highway which
had passed along High Street, South Bridge
Street and up Flowerhill. Thus New Cross
became the focal centre of the town, a mantle it
would wear today with greater distinction if
the streetscape were not apparently dedicated
wholly to the ignoble service of traffic
engineering.

George Arthur (1849-99) was
born in Airdrie High Street and
became apprenticed to James
Thomson, the leading architect
of the town. Later he formed an
association with William Baird,
forming the firm of Baird &
Arthur and in 1871 he took
charge of the business, *Mr
Baird by then being much
engaged in the coal trade*. In
1884 he began his own practice,
being appointed architect to the
Burgh the following year. He
later sampled the other side of
civic life by being elected
Provost for 1893-6. Arthur
Avenue remains named after
him. His eldest son, Colonel J
M Arthur followed his father
into the practice.

6 Scottish Power Showroom, Stirling Street,
1961, SSEB Architects
Largely timber framed with a handsome glazed
frontage and laminated portal beams, its roof
suspended below. The handling of the framing
and portal bolts has overtones of the Glasgow
Style.

Below *Airdrie Town Hall.*
Bottom *Airdrie Public Baths*

7 The Sir John Wilson Town Hall,
Stirling Street, 1912, James Thomson & Sons
The Town Hall was a gift to the town from the
then owner of the Airdrie estate. Pure civic
expression, a competition-winning classical
rectangle in creamy sandstone, the town crest
in a florid entablature over the door, the
baronial crest significantly higher between
Ionic columns just to show who was paying for
it. Still in use for its original purpose of hosting
public events, drama and concerts. Richly
ornamented interior.

8 Airdrie Public Baths, Stirling Street,
1935, J M Arthur
Handsome stripped classical masonry frontage
with recessed window bays and projecting
entrance tower: too restrained to compete with
its neighbours.

9 Black Bull Inn, 2 Alexander Street, 1899, J M Arthur (see p.50)
Characterful corner block with Glasgow Style touches in the pedimented entrances, sculptured stacks and bay with flat capped pinnacles. A rather resigned looking bovine supports the projecting bay over a splayed entrance.

Bank of Scotland, 10 Stirling Street, 1901, J M Arthur (see p.50)
Pleasantly asymmetrical composition of three storeys and attic in red sandstone, its bracketed balcony developing into a bay in Edwardian mode. Inset sculpture in the gable. Above its garish commercial signage, **11-15 Stirling Street**, *c*.1925, displays a frontage less despoiled than many in the street, its upper hall pedimented and columned, with Venetian windows with sandstone surrounds, its ashlar infilled with red brickwork. Stirling Street widens at this point to meet Graham Street and form New Cross.

Top *Black Bull Inn.*
Middle *Bank of Scotland.*
Above *11-15 Stirling Street*

Graham Street (*above*)
10 New Cross Corner, 1878, Baird & Arthur
Sweeps round the corner grandly into Bank Street to provide a setting for the Town House, the arms of Airdrie Burgh displayed high on a curved pediment. The strong rhythm of its rusticated sandstone upper bays diluted by street-level shops (see p.51).

Royal Bank of Scotland

11 Royal Bank of Scotland, 5 Graham Street
Smart mid-Victorian classical villa with two-storey Tuscan pilasters supporting a small central pediment. Pleasant rounded gable arches on either side shielding the rear service yard. Ashlar stonework now rouged in a decidedly unclassical pink.

Left and above Graham Street

12 Clydesdale Bank, 7 Graham Street,
1870, William Railton
Eccentric Jacobean, its rock-faced buff
sandstone towering over its neighbour, with
bold window details and ball-finialed dormers
whose rude exuberance fails to disguise an
ungainly composition.

Graham Street has a number of elegant 19th-
century stone frontages, almost to a man
diminished by crass shop signs and shopfitters'
disasters. **No 20 (Woolworths)** retains its
1936 art deco pilasters and arrowhead
decoration at first-floor level. The eastern end
of the street, victim of two phases of
redevelopment between 1970 and 1975, now
suffers from an overscaled office development
and supermarket which gaze vacantly at each
other from either side of the pedestrian
precinct.

Below Clydesdale Bank.
Bottom Airdrie Sheriff
Courthouse

13 Sheriff Courthouse, Graham Street,
1974, Lanark County Council Architects
Low flat-roofed block in white exposed
aggregate panels, decently landscaped. Green
slate-clad tower proclaims the entrance.

14 Broomfield Park Pavilion, Graham Street,
1907, James Shaw
Red brick home of Airdrieonians Football Club
(founded as Excelsior in 1878) which moved to
Broomfield in 1892; the glazed frontage a
modern addition.

Anderson Street
Anderson Street, named after John Anderson,
a member of the first Airdrie Town Council,
who had a tannery here beside the former
freestone quarry, curves pleasantly round from
Bank Street to the foot of Wellwynd, its 19th-
century frontages giving it the ambience of
some small county town (see p.49).

Airdrie Arts Centre

Scotland's first Free Library
*'Airdrie was the first town in
Scotland to adopt the Free
Libraries Act of 1853 - an
honour of which Airdrie can
never be robbed,'* Andrew
Carnegie
The Burgh of Airdrie adopted
the Free Libraries Act in 1853
and opened its first Library in
the Fiscal's room of Airdrie
Town Hall in 1856, many
volumes being provided from
the Library of Airdrie
Mechanics' Institution. The
expansion of its stock
necessitated its later removal to
Market Buildings before a
purpose-built town library was
jointly endowed by Dr
Carnegie, who had been greatly
impressed by Airdrie's
pioneering spirit, and by Sir
John Wilson to add to the
monies collected by public
subscription. It was constructed
in Anderson Street in 1893.

Right *Airdrie Post Office.*
Below *Airdrie Market*

Opposite: Middle top
Flowerhill Parish Church.
Middle bottom *Hallcraig Street.*
Bottom *Airdrie Town House*

15 **Airdrie Arts Centre**, Anderson Street, 1893,
George Arthur
Airdrie's first purpose-built library, largely
paid for by Andrew Carnegie. Delightful two-
storeyed classical temple in red sandstone.
Rusticated ashlar ground floor supports the
principal floor whose columns elevate a
handsome pediment, now much in need of
cleaning. Ionic columns at the entrance support
a curved entablature with the town crest
emblazoned there – only later, it was noticed,
carved irrevocably with the wrong Latin
inscription.

Burgh Police Offices, Anderson Street, 1959,
D Bruce
A competition-winning design in blond
sandstone, the green copper roof reflecting
Scandinavian influences.

16 **Airdrie Post Office**, Anderson Street, 1905,
W M Robertson
Fitting the modest scale of the street, the west
wing of its two storeys of red sandstone curved
to fit the site, twin pediments joined by a
balustrade. Now a resource centre.

Hallcraig Street
Once the line of the medieval King's Highway,
later lined with thatched weavers' cottages:
now an emaciated avenue with gap sites and
car parks.

Airdrie Market, Hallcraig Street, 1856,
James Thomson
Harled gushet building, entrance signified by
diapered pilasters rising to support a central
pediment, flanked by chimneys with the town
crest grandly aloft.

17 St Margaret's RC Church, Hallcraig Street, 1839, Wilkie & Gray (*right*)
Simple neo-classical church whose square tower and octagonal spire rises above a pedimented front with giant Tuscan pilasters. A welcome relief from the regiment of Gothic churches soon to advance on the Monklands, its style was due to the Bishop's desire for a *modern* church. Prior to its construction, for a time, Airdrie adherents had to travel to St Andrew's in Glasgow for services, many accomplishing this on foot.

18 St Andrew's Hospice, Hallcraig Street, 1986, Oberlander Associates (*above*)
Low cottage-like courtyard hospice like a self-contained village in well-disciplined dark stained timbers and brickwork (see p.70).

19 Flowerhill Parish Church, Wilson Street, 1874, Matthew Forsyth (see p.52)
Church, campanile, manse and hall are all combined in one complex, all dominated by the tall arcaded campanile. Its green Roman tiled roof replaced the original vertiginous slated spire which was much more Germanic in character. The church is positively Romanesque with a splendid plate-traceried wheel window in the east gable.

Bank Street
20 Airdrie Town House, 1826, Alexander Baird
A very neat town house containing a prison, police office and a good town hall, Baird chosen in preference to George Waddell. The most distinguished building in Airdrie when first constructed, this delightful classical cube is ennobled by its three-stage clock tower and spire. Pairs of Tuscan columns identify the entrance. An imposing symbol of authority amidst the weavers' cottages, the laying of its foundation stone was sufficiently important to warrant the purchase of a new blue coat for the Town Crier and Criminal Officer, for hitherto the venue for public meetings in Airdrie had been one of the malt barns. Within a few years

13

Right *County Buildings.*
Above *Commercial
Development, Bank Street*

Peden

RCAHMS

Below *Royal Bank of Scotland.*
Middle top *Anderson Street
gushet block.* Middle bottom
Claude Alexandre, Mill Loan

Peden

Monklands District Council

Monklands District Council

Monklands District Council

the Town House would see service as both a
cholera hospital and a barracks. In 1854 the
Fiscal's room was shelved to allow its use as
Scotland's first free library.

County Buildings, 1858, James Thomson
Suffered so chronically from subsidence that
they have now given way (literally) to an
eyecatching development in pink blockwork by
the Cunningham Glass Partnership, 1990.

Royal Bank of Scotland, Bank Street,
1874, James Thomson
Impressive banker's classical: well-composed
façade in honey-coloured sandstone, framed by
slightly projecting end pavilions. Pedimented
windows at first floor, with arms of George I
appearing improbably from the central broken
pediment, emphasise the principal floor.
Ferociously carved lions' heads peer down from
the bracketed eaves. The clashing granite base
and aluminium windows reflect a later lapse in
taste.
　　Bank Street runs into **South Bridge Street**,
Anderson Street, **Mill Loan** and **Hallcraig
Street** all within the space of a few yards, the
gushet with Anderson Street being a handsome
curved block of 1870, that with Mill Loan, an
angular drapers in '30s style by Whyte & Nicol,
both face Airdrie Market.

Bank of Scotland, South Bridge Street, 1846,
J Smith (*left*)
Plain symmetrical elegance in two storeys of
polished ashlar with deeply moulded window
surrounds, string-course and dentilled
entrance above a Doric-columned entrance. Its
distinguished character, in the company of the
other 19th-century frontages, rebukes the
strident commercialism that has overwhelmed
the rest of the street.

21 **Ebenezer Congregational Church**,
Broomknoll Street, 1882, James Thomson
Replaces the original church of 1836 built after
a secession from Wellwynd. Rudimentary
Gothic in buff sandstone, entered through its
western gable, the square belltower and spire
identifying the corner.

22 **Broomknoll Parish Church**, Broomknoll
Street, 1888, James Davidson
Tall, spikily gabled barn which, lacking a spire,
makes do with a vestigial battlemented tower,
pinnacled in the Decorated style. Finely carved
relief panel over the entrance.

23 **Airdrie Masonic Lodge**, Broomknoll Street,
1980, James Davidson & Son
Inscrutable dark brick box, the high rear
section pinnacled like a place of worship, the
roof sweeping down to the street frontage,
wrapped in a big copper-clad fascia.

24 **Housing Department Offices**, Broomknoll
Street, 1900, Alexander McGregor Mitchell
Red sandstone confection of oriel window, gable
and turret dominated by an over-scaled hooded
entrance flanked by Corinthian pilasters. Self-
confident civic building of the period, originally
constructed as offices for Airdrie Water Board,
the town crest effusively carved high on the
end gable (*below*).

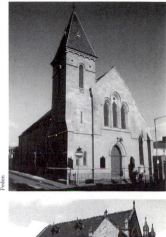

Top *Ebenezer Church*. Above
Broomknoll Parish Church

25 **Old Cross**
Former centre of the village from the early
18th century, although none of the thatched
cottages which filled the Laird's feus survives.
Its generous width is under-exploited as a piece
of townscape, and wasted as a crossroads.

James Thomson (1822-98)
whose father was a weaving
agent and Airdrie Town
Councillor, initially began an
apprenticeship as a joiner in
1837. His scholarly interests
led him to travel nightly to
Coatbridge for lessons in
draughtsmanship, and he
eventually obtained his
architectural diploma in
Edinburgh in 1846. Shortly
afterwards, he was
commissioned to design the
New Monkland Poorhouse.
Designs followed for the
Courthouse in Bank Street,
Hallcraig Market and Airdrie
Public Hall, and in 1874 his
Royal Bank of Scotland was
completed. Perhaps his most
notable contribution to the
county was his designs for over
25 schools and a number of
churches.

26 Fruitfield, East High Street, *c.*1880, J Thomson
Bold Italianate villa, replacing the house of William Mack, first Provost of Airdrie, which faces south over what was once the Provost's orchard, the prospect rudely interrupted by a gasometer. **Nanny Boyd's Seminary**, a thatched cottage built in 1706 to provide rudimentary schooling for the children of the hamlet, stood at the north end of the garden. High Victorian **Bank House**, adjacent, with its pavilion roof, paired windows, vermiculated quoins, would be an appropriate house for a bank manager. Its stables turn the corner into Chapel Street, where the original hayloft door survives high in the boundary wall.

27 Glencruitten, 27 Chapel Street, is a two-storey Greek villa distinguished by its architraves at the entrance and bold window surrounds.

28 The corner block, which punctuates the 19th-century terraced frontage of **East High Street**, is an effusively decorated piece of Victorian confectionery by J Thomson, scrolls over the doors, big Jacobean skew-puts with ball finials, culminating in twin-bracketed chimneys and a central anthemion-capped oculus. Its impact diluted by regrettable shopfront alterations.

29 Parochial Board Offices, North Bridge Street, 1892, George Arthur
Pretty, smart little building: four bays at ground level transformed into three upstairs by the dominating, pediment-corbelled bay which surges up through a balustrade. Two storeys of delightful red sandstone with half-engaged Ionic columns. A fine interior existed until its conversion to **Children's Panel Offices** for Strathclyde Regional Council.

Top *Bank House*. Middle top *Bank House stables*. Middle bottom *27 Chapel Street*. Above *East High Street corner*

The old High Street was reputedly the site of **Tibbie Tamson's Change House**, where Charles Edward Stuart and his officers lodged when their Highlanders billeted themselves on the village during the '45. His troops drank the village dry before moving on to Glasgow, and no bills were paid. Tibbie afterwards remarked that she *would raither hae a chapman's groat than a prince's promises*.

Parochial Board Offices

30 **Lodge Bar**, High Street
Pantomime Scots Baronial frontage tacked on
to an 18th-century building: exaggeratedly
crowstepped twin gables to the road, window
surrounds ambitiously surmounted by scrolled
decoration.

AIRDRIE: North
31 **St Margaret's Secondary School**,
Waverley Drive, 1975,
Strathclyde Region Architects
Large, geometric brick and glass school
dominating **Rawyards Park**, its four- and
five-storey classroom block and ancillary wings
stepping down the hillside like a ziggurat.

32 **Monklands Leisure Centre**, Motherwell
Street, 1978, extended 1990, Monklands
District Architects with Matheson Gleave
A piece of fun; though some would have it as
black humour. A large ebony corrugated box
fronted by red and buff striped cladding, a
yellow-framed barrel-vaulted arcade and much
decorative brickwork. A veritable liquorice
allsort (see p.50).

33 **Sheltered Housing**, Milton Street, 1985,
McGurn Logan Duncan & Opfer
A fine west-facing site is well exploited in
designer roughcast with adventurous
minimalist entrance porches. Economic
construction here graced with a spare sense
of style.

Top *Lodge Bar*. Middle top *St
Margaret's Secondary School.*
Middle bottom *Monklands
Leisure Centre.* Above *Milton
Street Sheltered Housing*

Drumgelloch
34 **Drumbathie Road Villas**, 1920s, J M Arthur
Four fine houses: **Pinecrest**, **Rockpark**,
Woodcroft and **Glentore**. The last of these
(renamed **Thornton House**) was built for the
architect himself, and not surprisingly is the

Left and below *Drumbathie
Road Villas*

most interesting. White, pavilion-roofed and turreted, this L-plan house exemplifies how the second Scots revival developed between the wars into a search for a new Scots style.

35 St Paul's Episcopal Church, Springwells Avenue, 1897, H D Walton
Victorian Gothic, gable end to the road, hall to the·rear, all in attractive bull-faced pink ashlar with polished dressings. The adjacent **parsonage** by George Arthur.

Thrashbush

36 Airdrie Academy, South Commonhead Avenue, 1941, J S Stewart (*left*)
One of many projects of the late 1930s which was interrupted by the Second World War, not being completed until a decade later by the County Architect for Lanarkshire. Principal classroom blocks are in an inverted Y-plan with a central courtyard, a rather grim three-storey affair with a narrow structural grid of columns, imposing only in sheer scale (see p.69).

37 Arran View, off Commonhead Street, 1867, Alexander Thomson (see p.49)
Thomson massing and details evident from the three-storey tower, battered plinths, incised ornament and shallow pitched roofs with generous overhangs. Built for Gavin Black Motherwell, an Airdrie Town Councillor and later Provost, it bears marked similarities to Tor House at Rothesay, which Thomson designed about the same time. Allowed to fall into dereliction, the original interiors largely lost, before being converted to flats by Ian Bridges in 1987, whose new houses in buff concrete blocks with Thomsonesque detail in

Below & right *Arran View*

the garden serve to underscore the genius of the original.

The adjacent **Viewbank** is a merchant villa of similar date in classic style, **Assumption House** (Arran House) an even larger Italianate villa adjoining, bearing a strange modernist extension by Jack Coia, built as a chapel.

38 **Thornhill**, a bijou Baronial villa in Commonhead Street, has crowstepped dormer windows and a ball finial poised invitingly above a central pedimented dormer.

Chapelside Primary School,
Chapel Street, 1883, George Arthur
Something of a Baronial *tour-de-force*. Commandingly set above its playground, this E-plan, single-storey school is flanked by projecting wings in buff sandstone framing a triple gabled centrepiece. A grandeur of detail normally reserved for grander buildings: corners are corbelled over rounded arrises, machicolations, crowstepped gables, a pyramidal-roofed bellcote and much more. Extended by George Arthur in 1885 and James Thomson & Sons in 1905: now used as an educational resource centre.

Top *Thornhill*. Above & left *Chapelside Primary School*

AIRDRIE: East
Clark Street
Stretching east from the town centre, Clark Street, like Alexander Street, has a procession of substantial south-facing Victorian villas, the bijou villas and terraced properties opposite having to endure the less-favoured north aspect for their entrances, with the railway to the rear.

Lingley Lodge, on the toffs' side of the avenue, is sub-Thomson in design, its oversailing roof with an anthemion leaf sprouting from the gable. The more Gothic **Registrar's Office**, opposite, has an entrance reminiscent of turn-of-the-century railway architecture. The adjacent streets of **Springhill** and **Springwells** echo these middle-class stone archetypes in some variety. **North Biggar Road** (formed in the 17th century as the only major north/south

Below *Clark Street*.
Bottom *Lingley Lodge*

thoroughfare in Airdrie by the Flemings of Cumbernauld, as a link to their Biggar estates) 39 contains **Stanley House** (see p.52), a fine single-storey classical villa of *c*.1812, its entrance grandly emphasised by twinned Doric columns at the portico. The gardens house part of the once magnificent 1636 entrance gateway from Old College, Glasgow (see *Central Glasgow* in this series) (see p.52).

The corner at the eastern extremity of Clark Street is neatly turned by the compact **Queen** 40 **Victoria Nurses Home**, 1904, by J M Arthur, in roughcast with red sandstone dressings and hints of Glasgow Style, its red-tiled roof making it speak with a rather English accent.

Carlisle Road was formed *c*.1820 as the main highway to Stirling from the south. The **bonded warehouses** which front it at 41 **Craigneuk**, known locally as the *Spitfire Factory*, were constructed by the Airdrie transport king, John C Sword, the founder of Western SMT, as a garage for part of his fleet of 400 motor buses. They were later converted into a wartime factory for aviation parts, its main production devoted to the fabrication of wing sections for Hurricane fighter aircraft.

Top *Stanley House.*
Above *Old College gateway*

Below *Croft Park.*
Bottom *109 Forrest Street*

Forrest Street
Succession of late Victorian villas in their own 42 grounds the larger facing south, **Croft Park** the most impressive: two storeys of solid merchant material in Italianate buff sandstone. The quality runs out abruptly as the road leads to the east, although **No 109** by James Hamilton is a rather interesting villa of sub-1930s influence, a glazed band of windows at first-floor level sweeping round from south to west over a splayed corner; in local and belated imitation of the International Style. 46 The enormous **Clarkston Primary School** by J Stewart, County Architect, has three pediments to the road frontage hung with vertical timbers, lending a hint of incongruous Tudor.

The inter-war council house terraces of 47 **Forrest Street** and **Katherine Street**, by Alex Thomson of J Thomson & Sons, display commendable solidity and symmetry, ashlar panels at ground floor offset with roughcast above, topped with crowstepped gables.

Grahamshill Street
43 **Redcraig**, 1909, by James Shaw, is an Edwardian Arts & Crafts villa of some style

with its swept roofs and dormers and
44 overhanging eaves; **Sherwood**, a splendid if
eccentric Gothic bungalow complete with
battlements and Robin of Barnesdale's bow and
45 quiver on its armorial panel; **Annfield**, a
delightful Regency villa, with a generously
scrolled portico and bold overstated quoins
giving it considerable presence; **Earlston** to
the west has a remarkable porch with
solomonic columns.

Left *Redcraig*. Top *Annfield*.
Above *Earlston*

Below *Clarkston Parish
Church*. Middle *Wester Moffat
House*. Bottom *Boots plc Offices*

CLARKSTON
48 **Clarkston Parish Church**,
Church Crescent, 1837
A simple galleried box-kirk in local rubble
behind a straightforward Gothic gabled façade
in ashlar, now almost obscured by its little
avenue of trees. A bellcote sits at the apex of
the gable with matching finials on the skew
stones.

49 **Wester Moffat House**, Towers Road, 1862,
Charles Wilson
Splendid and energetically massed Baronial
mansion built for William Towers-Clark not
unlike Wilson's Baronial villa in Dundee (see
Dundee in this series). Full repertoire of
crowsteps, battlemented towers, pinnacles and
corbelled turrets with fishtail slating. The
original buff sandstone, almost unrecognisably
blackened as a legacy of the area's industrial
past, came by a temporary railway from the
source of the sandstone, a pit owned by the
Springbank Coal Co, to the house, a distance of
about one-and-a-half miles: part of **Wester
Moffat Hospital**.

RAWYARDS
50 **Boots plc Offices**, Motherwell Street, 1949,
Boots Architects Department
The first tangible signs of regeneration after

the demise of Airdrie's traditional industries. Two long storeys in local ashlar focused upon an entry tower, a little bland but impressively scaled.

51 Rawyards House, Motherwell Street, 1880, James Thomson & Sons
Designed for Mr Motherwell this was *a commodious mansion house on the site of its predecessor*. It is indeed commodious. A large two-storey villa, it faces south with some Italianate detail and a rather idiosyncratic composition of bays and wings, the windows with big sprocketed cills, other details reminiscent of the (unrelated) Alexander Thomson who had designed nearby **Arran View** for Motherwell's son a decade earlier. Now a nursing home.

Below & right *Rawyards House*

AIRDRIE: South
52 Alexandra Primary School, Cairnhill Road, 1849
The original Airdrie Academy, erected through the magnanimity of Mr Alexander of Airdrie House to provide a successor to the basic burgh school in Wellwynd, much extended in 1887 by A McGregor Mitchell in a similarly lacklustre Victorian idiom for Queen Victoria's Jubilee.
Academy Street, a little pocket of late-19th-
53 century cottages, has **Carrick** and **Annick**, a pair of semi-detached villas, ostensibly single-storey but with upper rooms lit by bay windows set into arched niches in each gable. It was an area of considerable industrial activity (most of
54 the sites now cleared and vacant), and **Hogg Street** retains one of two of the examples of Victorian works buildings in red engineering brickwork. **Arthur Avenue**, opposite, climbs away from the grime of industry with a solid middle-class suburb of stone villas.
55 Beaconsfield, Victoria Place, is Greek,

Hogg Street

sporting ornate chimney stalks. **Swiss Cottage**, Victoria Place, is florid in Victorian romantic mode. **Woodville**, 1897, George Arthur, dominated by its two-storey circular bay (see p.69); **Flowerhill Manse**, asymmetrically Italianate, **Dalmagarry**, 1897, George Arthur, and **Cairnbaan**, an interesting double villa built for John Orr of John Orr & Sons. The little gem at the top of the hill is the **Anchorage**, a miniature château by James Shaw, decorated presumably for a seafarer.

CAIRNHILL

58 **Cairnhill House**, Cairnhill Road, 1841, John Baird

A bold mansion house in exaggerated Jacobean designed by Baird while Alexander Thomson was his apprentice (to whom its crispness might be attributed). A feast of strapwork and finials, which encased John Craig's Georgian house of the 1760s at the rear. In Russia, it

Left *Anchorage*. Top *Swiss Cottage*. Middle *Woodville*. Above *Cairnbaan*

Left *Cairnhill House*. Below *Cairnhill Doocot*

Cairnhill is almost where the industrialisation of the Monklands started. David Mushet, the manager of Calder ironworks discovered the blackband ironstone (iron nodules in a matrix of coal-like material) on the Cairnhill estate in 1801. This was the material which was to make Coatbridge the *Iron Burgh*, though it was 1828 before the technology to exploit it became available, when J B Neilson of Glasgow Gas Works discovered and rapidly patented the hot-blast furnace for iron smelting, which reduced dramatically the amount of coal required in the process, and thus the costs. The piratical Bairds of Gartsherrie took out licence to use this new furnace, but refused to pay any royalties. By the time that due process of law had caught up with their breach of patent, they had profited so much through it that the compensatory damages of £11,876 and £40,000 costs could be paid without a second thought. In fact, the Bairds rather typically negotiated a discount for paying immediately in cash.

might have been beautifully restored by the state to honour the working-class craftsmen who gave it life; in Scotland it crumbled picturesquely into dereliction and was demolished in 1991.

59 **Doocot** (see p.49) and **Stables**, Sutherland Drive, 1762, by John Craig, form an excellent cylindrical cot with an ogee slated roof, the flight holes protected under the eaves, almost the double of the now demolished Daldowie doocot. The cot forms the centrepiece of the north wall of a two-storey courtyard range, recently demolished and rebuilt in something of their original form as domestic accommodation.

ROCHSOLLOCH

60 **Rochsolloch Farm**, Victoria Place
Commendable renovation by Creanor & Marshall of a 19th-century farmhouse and steading with a number of new houses in pleasantly related form and materials.

Top right Cairnhill Doocot and Stables. Below and right Rochsolloch Farm

BSC Imperial Works Offices

61 **BSC Imperial Works Offices**, Victoria Place, 1977, Reiach and Hall (see p.70)
Award-winning sophisticated administrative suite, giving the steelworks a high-technology entrance. The pair of elegantly steel-framed pavilions which step down their sloping site are colourfully massed in red brickwork with a yellow framed grid of cladding, standing out against the gigantic grey backdrop of the works sheds, the largest of which covers fifteen acres of the hillside.

62 Victoria Industrial Estate, Rochsolloch Road, 1986, Building Design Partnership
Courtyard of gleaming silver and blue sheds for small business, roofscapes enlivened by glazed barrel vaults at the apex, and matching glazed eaves.

Above *Victoria Industrial Estate.* Left *Rochsolloch Primary School*

This was **Ruchsallach**, the *hill of the willows*, in the 17th century, home of the Crawfurds of Ruchsallach. The estate was later extensively exploited for coal. By 1840 the Rochsolloch estate alone contained 11 pits, two mines and two open-cast collieries.

63 Rochsolloch Primary School,
Kippen Street, 1899, James Shaw
Winner of a limited competition held by Airdrie School Board, it has much in common with the earlier Chapelside School, displaying a purposefully detailed muddle of crowsteps, hoodmoulds and similar details: even the soil vent pipes are crowned with thistles.

The Aitchisons of Rochsolloch
The Aitchison family purchased Rochsolloch estates in 1685, but later diversified their investments abroad. John Aitchison leased sugar plantations in the West Indies, evidently a lucrative trade: in 1780 the chattels of his Grenada plantation were assessed and it was recorded that the *total value of negroes, slaves and horses* was £21,183.

His daughters, the three Misses Aitchison, eventually resided at Airdrie House and showed unanimity in bequeathing the Rochsolloch and Airdrie estates to their nephew Sir William Alexander, Chief Baron of the Exchequer in England.

WHINHALL
64 Monklands District General Hospital,
Monkscourt Avenue, 1977,
Keppie, Henderson & Partners
A simple layered composition of horizontal banded rectangular blocks of concrete panels alternating with black-framed glazing set in the fine parkland site of former grounds of Airdrie House (seat of the Hamiltons of Airdrie).

Below *Monklands District Hospital.* Left *Airdrie House*

65 Airdrie War Memorial, Mulvey Crescent, 1922, J M Arthur
A simple cenotaph in grey granite on a raised dais, standing between **Centenary Park** and **West End Park**. Winner of a local competition judged by J J Burnet.

Above *Airdrie War Memorial.*
Right *Gushet House, Alexander Street (now demolished)*

(1) *Meadowfield.* (2) *Ralston Street.* (3) *Victoria Primary School.* (4) *Rullion Green*

Alexander Street offers villadom of the late Victorian period, visible evidence of the success of Airdrie's industrial growth. Smaller properties on the south side had to back on to the railway, while the larger merchant villas to the north enjoyed the view such as **Earlsferry**, **66**
67 1881, **St Fillans**, and **Meadowfield** – in the Greek style, its curved bay complemented by leaded glass of the period. The adjacent **Ralston Street** has an early pair of semi-detached bungalows with sprocketed eaves and other quirky details by Archie Revie.

68 Victoria Primary School, Aitchison Street, 1932, J Stewart, County Architect
A formidable structure in ashlar with roughcast upper panels, its plan in the form of a hollow square with four corner towers.

69 Ferguson House, 107 Aitchison Street, 1877
An imposing Italianate villa in two storeys of buff sandstone originally with a clear view to Cairnhill, its entrance front with incised Vitruvian scroll decoration. Now a nursing home. **Rullion Green**, 109 Aitchison Street, **70** 1906, J M Arthur, in red sandstone, has a trio of half-timbered dormer windows, its leaded glazing profuse with swagged motifs, facing north over the extensive Whinhall estates.

GLENMAVIS
New Monkland Kirk, Condorrat Road, 1777,
Andrew Bell (see p.71)
The disjunction of the parishes of Old and New
Monkland in 1655, produced a primitive single-
storey rectangular kirk with a heather-thatch
roof and a partly earthen floor. A steeple was
added in 1698 with a prison cell at the disposal
of the kirk session. It soon suffered so badly
from overcrowding that *youthful members of
the congregation colonised the exposed joists to
roost*. The heritors met in 1776 to approve
plans drawn up by Andrew Bell of Airdrie for a
new kirk, retaining only the original steeple.
Alternative plans by James Muir were rejected
because his design could not hold the 1200
seats which had been specified. *Rustic corners*
were added as an afterthought at an extra cost
of £6, and for a further £6 the old steeple
(which contains a doocot) was repaired. The
result is a fine Old Scots plain kirk, well
worthy of its commanding position at the
highest point of the village. There is a simple
watchhouse by the cemetery and a number of
interesting gravestones dating back to the 17th
century. The apse was added in 1904 by John
Arthur.

New Monkland Kirk

The Gerards of Rochsoles
John Gerard of Rochsoles
(1765-1824), the brother of
Alexander Gerard the
Himalayan explorer, was the
first of a line of Indian army
officers to own the Rochsoles
estate. His nephew Montagu
Gerard latterly inherited the
policies and, following
campaigns in Egypt and
Afghanistan as commander of a
cavalry regiment, developed
some reputation as a tiger
hunter, eventually hanging the
interior of Rochsoles House
with the spreadeagled evidence
of his marksmanship.

Left *Rochsoles Stables.*
Above *Rochsoles House*

Rochsoles Stables, Raebog Road, 1839
A U-shaped range which may once have been
symmetrical around its central doocot and twin
stable wings, now much altered. All that
remains of the great estate of William
Cochrane of Rouchsoills and later the Gerard
family, an estate which originated when the
Monklands was still a single parish.

PLAINS
The centre of a group of mining hamlets on the
moorland to the east of Airdrie – Ballochney,
Arden, Meadowhead, Stanrigg and Whiterigg –
all of which have subsequently vanished along
with the pits which formed them. Stanrigg was
the scene of a great pit disaster in 1918 when

St David's Church

19 men and boys were entombed by an inrush of the wet peat moss. Eleven of them were never recovered. A plot of open ground among the open-cast excavations which cover the area marks their isolated resting place.

St David's Church, Meadowhead Road, 1950, Gillespie Kidd & Coia
One of a series of long-plan standard types which developed post-war. Corrugated industrial roof and cast stone frontage declare this to be very much an economy model. Now threatened with demolition.

71 **Brownieside**, Airdrie Road, *c.*1870, J Thomson
The laird's house, former home of the Tennant family, facing the village in the reduced circumstances of a List D school. A handsome buff sandstone Italianate villa of the late Victorian period, it has been extended, the west wing containing an art deco interior.

Right *Brownieside.* Below *Easter Moffat House.* Middle *Greystones Farm.* Bottom *Detail of Doocot*

Meadowhead House, Ballochney Road, Whiterigg, Joseph Cowan
Four-square Victorian villa in bull-faced sandstone, a former presbytery, commanding fine vistas to the south-west and virtually the last vestige of this once-thriving mining community. Its adjacent **school** and **chapel school**, 1900, also by J Cowan, lies derelict.

Easter Moffat House, Brownieside Road, *c.*1830
Tudor mansion set in its own parkland, with just enough mouldings and finials to impress. Now recast as a golf clubhouse, much of the original interiors surviving. Its U-shaped stable block, **Greystones Farm**, adjoins: a fourth side enclosed by screen walls. Entered through a pend beneath the central tower which houses the doocot, its gables pleasingly ornamented with ball finials. Now converted to domestic use.

LONGRIGGEND

One of the largest of Airdrie's satellite mining communities in Victorian times, set high on a moorland ridge, commanding fine views north-west to the Campsie Fells. Open-cast coal is still worked here giving the landscape a rather tormented look, and further depredations are caused by the extraction of peat from the moss on a commercial basis. Of the hundred houses in the village a century ago, when coal was king, only a handful remain.

Longriggend Parish Church,

Telegraph Road, *c.*1880, George Arthur
A petite Gothic Revival kirk, nicely detailed arched entrance, gable to the road with simple lancet windows and a bellcote over. Adjacent manse of 1889.

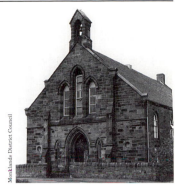

Above Longriggend Parish Church

CALDERCRUIX

This village has an industrial past quite different from the rest of the Monklands in that it owes its existence to the proprietors of Caldercruix Paper Mills and Textile Printing Works who started construction work here in 1848 to harness the North Calder Water. It drove two of the largest water wheels in Scotland in the production of high-quality papers and a renowned blotting paper. The mill owners built much of the community, with a more generous paternalism than that of the ironfounders and coal owners of the Monklands. The 1891 mill is now demolished. The **Craig Institute**, Airdrie Road, 1908, by J M Arthur, was founded by the mill to provide dining facilities, recreation and a library for the workforce. It now faces the vacant mill site. The entrance to the Craig Institute, two storeys of blond sandstone in rather perfunctory Baronial style with crowsteps, is now converted to housing.

Caldercruix Mills (*left*)

In 1846, the three sons of a Newbattle paper manufacturer, Thomas, Robert and George Craig, acquired ground beside the river at Caldercruix along with rights to use the soft water from Hillend Reservoir, which had originally been constructed to provide water for the Forth & Clyde Canal, in a new papermaking enterprise. The success of Caldercruix No 6 paper effectively formed the Caldercruix community and incidentally maintained the link with Newbattle which the monks had formed seven centuries earlier. The mill owners built their own workers' housing in the village as well as the Craig Institute which contained the mill dining rooms and library and endowed the Craig Memorial Church.

Craig Institute

Caldercruix Parish Church, Main Street, 1890, A McGregor Mitchell (see p.70)
Simple twin-aisled box kirk in a Gothic Revival overcoat, given character by its squat crowstepped belltower and four octagonal pinnacles rising over stepped corner buttresses. Spacious interior is illumined by a series of fine Glasgow Style wrought-iron candelabra.
Caldercruix Home Farm adjacent, the farmhouse rather unusually replaced *c*.1880 by an Italianate villa (old steading to the rear).

Free Church, Airdrie Road, 1896, J Arthur
Badly damaged by fire, now surviving as Lodge Caldercruix St John No 1314 with its original spire much truncated, looking rather isolated.

The **Public School**, Airdrie Road, 1875, by A McGregor Mitchell, is an imposing gabled building in dark whinstone with light sandstone dressings, now transformed into an **Outdoor Education Centre** (*below*).

Top *Caldercruix Parish Church from the top of the mill chimney.* Above *Caldercruix Free Church*

Robert Haldane of Auchengray (1764-1842)
Robert Haldane of Airthrey purchased Auchengray estate in 1809, its windswept 2400 acres then boasting only a single tree. Following distinguished service in the Royal Navy where he took part in the relief of Gibraltar, he followed his personal mission to aid the spread of the gospel in India, a task which found little support in the East India Company or indeed the Church of Scotland. Evidently displaying remarkable power as a gentleman preacher and writer on controversial religious subjects, this kenspeckle figure in his long powdered wig led a significant religious revival in Switzerland and France during 1816 and subsequently was known to preach to his assembled tenantry at Auchengray in a chapel built over the granary. Attendance, one imagines, may not have been optional.

Eastercroft, Airdrie Road, *c*.1900, J M Crawford (*above*)
Built to survey the endless source of power for the mills, Caldercruix mill owner's mansion beside **Hillend Reservoir** has been variously extended. A solid pile of ashlar, rather impressive in a restrained Scots Arts & Crafts

idiom, not dissimilar to the early work of Lorimer. Now a nursing home. Also, gauntly looking out over Hillend Reservoir from the north, **Auchengray** is the deteriorating shell of a neo-classical mansion of the 1820s, extended with bays in 1924 by J M Arthur and, gutted by fire in 1937, open to the winds ever since.

SALSBURGH

Isolated mining village which grew around ironstone and coal deposits, extracted by the Coltness Iron Company. Salsburgh's unhappy look is the consequence of the old A8 trunk road splitting the inter-war housing scheme from the Main Street. **Nos 149-155** remain as examples of the simple miners' cottages which once lined it. Edwardian **Shottskirk Public School**, School Road (the M8 its closest neighbour), James Cowie, 1911, is enlivened by a few Glasgow Style touches. **Salsburgh Chapel**, at the eastern end of the village, is '30s suburban style by Alexander McNally in 1937, a little cross-plan bungalow chapel in roughcast with red brick dressings and a red tiled roof.

Top *Auchengray.*
Above *149-155 Main Street, Salsburgh*

Left *Salsburgh Chapel.* Below *Blackhill Transmitter Station*

Blackhill Transmitter Station, Duntilland Road, 1988, BBC Architects
In the long shadow of the Kirk o' Shotts transmitter aerial to the south. Its fine details in red brickwork, with corbelled window surrounds and splayed heads at upper floor level, look slightly incongruous in its fiercely exposed high moorland setting.

SHOTTSBURN
Shottsburn Church, 1771
A simple harled box kirk with adjacent manse lies neglected and in seemingly terminal condition in Hirst Road, its name deriving from a *shot,* which was the measure of a rig-length

of ground in the runrig system in use here until the early 18th century. Its construction was prompted by a secession in the parish following the forced settlement of the Revd David Orr as minister at Kirk o' Shotts in 1738. At least Orr's ordination dinner appears to have been a success, the 43 in attendance enjoying 61 bottles of claret, 4 of spirits and 8 casks of ale.

Top *Shottsburn.*
Above *Kirk o' Shotts*

High frequency 'triffid' at Kirk o' Shotts

Kirk o' Shotts, Hirst Road, 1821, (see p.50)
James Gillespie Graham with James Brash
A symbol of the cauld blast of Presbyterianism on this bleak and windswept hill, the elevated position making its striking silhouette the best known in the Monklands. Built on the site of a chapel founded by Archibald the Grim, Earl of Douglas, in 1450 and dedicated to St Catherine of Sienna. This simple freestone rectangle is distinguished by four Gothic traceried windows in each flank which flood the interior with light and a small pinnacled bellcote at the apex of the entrance gable above crowsteps (the original spire being struck by lightning and destroyed in 1876). *Mr Gillespie, of Edinburgh, got £50 for the plan which was modified by Mr Brash at a little additional cost*, the contractor, John Loudon of Airdrie, was paid £2518. One of the oldest stones in the kirkyard (see p.49) commemorates William Smith of Mormellen, a Covenanter, who was attacked and murdered nearby on his way home from the Pentland Rising of 1666. Between 1760 and 1835, the isolated kirkyard was much troubled by Resurrection Men (as medical grave robbers

became known) and watches had to be posted.

A later minister commented that the parish suffered each year 9 months of winter and 3 of very wet weather.

The better known BBC transmitter aerial of the same name rises into the heavens about a mile to the east of the Kirk.

CHAPELHALL

The 15th-century Newbattle monks dedicated a chapel to St Catherine, which lay at the junction of Burniebrae Road and Carlisle Road. Until the onset of the blast furnaces and iron working in the 1830s, it was, with its associated **Monk Mill** on the **North Calder Water**, all that existed here. The industrial revolution demanded rapid expansion, bringing blast furnaces, but they have long been replaced by a sprawling industrial estate. The earliest buildings date from the mid 19th century.

Chapelhall Parish Church, Russell Street, 1857

Cruciform if unexciting Gothic executed in a mixture of styles, with an adjacent manse which dates from the 1860s. Its square tower rises into an unusual octagonal belfry with an abrupt, rather Byzantine copper cap, suggesting a later truncation of the original spire.

St Aloysius's Church, Main Street, 1884, Pugin & Pugin

A rather standard church from the Pugin &

Bartram de Shotts, the robber giant

Bartram was a bandit of great stature and supposedly a match for a dozen men. His depredations in the Shotts area during the late 14th century became so outrageous that Robert II offered a reward of a hawk's flight of land for Bartram's head. The Laird of Muirhead duly obliged after a cunning ambush and thus gained a charter over the lands of Shotts. His descendant, Muirhead of Lachop, later fell on Flodden Field along with Hamilton, the Laird of Airdrie.

Before the king in order stood
The stout Laird of Muirhead
Wi' that sam' twa hand muckle
sword
That Bartram fell'd stark deid
Twa hundred mair of his ain name
Frae Torwood and the Clyde
Sware they would ne'er gang to hame
But all die by his side
Many a bloody claw they dealt
The like was never seen
And had nae that braw leader fal'n
They ne'er had slain the king.

Sir Walter Scott, *The Ballad of the Battle of Flodden Field*

Left *St Aloysius's Church.* Below *Chapelhall Parish Church*

72 The site of **Monkland House** (*below*), now overrun by a speculative housing development, lies to the north of the industrial estate in a glen below Monkland Bridge. A splendid palace of the early 17th century to judge by its description – *a large bodie of a house with two jambs* (wings) *and four rounds* (towers) – it was built by Sir James Cleland of Monkland upon the Lands of Peddersburne. It suffered a number of fires during its chequered history, two conflagrations within a month being enough to seal its fate.

Pugin pattern book, distinguished by an unusually splendid rose window facing the street. An interior of some quality, including a mosaic-decorated marble reredos at the high altar. The **Presbytery** (*left and above*), 1934, by Alexander McNally of Glasgow, lies behind the church to exploit fine views to the west; a stylish 1930s villa, the red rustic brickwork of the ground floor offset by painted wet-dash roughcast to the upper. Much original period interior, including a panelled dining room and moderne bathroom.

CALDERBANK

The district around the Faskine coal workings was industrialised earlier than most of the Monklands. Coals were shipped to Glasgow as soon as the eastern section of the Monklands Canal was opened in 1792, and forgemasters set up on the bank of the Calder shortly afterwards, thus earning Calderbank the name of *The Monklands Forge*. From 1800 into the 1930s, Calderbank was effectively a company village, in the ownership of the succession of industrialists who ran the Calderbank Iron & Steel works. Many of them operated the infamous *truck* system of payment, by which the bulk of their workers' wages were paid not in cash, but in the form of goods and credit vouchers which could be redeemed only in the company store. But this was hardly the New Lanark store and there was little evidence of Robert Owen's co-operative system in Calderbank's hard regime. Child labour was rife, miners' sons following their fathers down the pits from the age of ten onwards; prior to the 1842 Mines Act it was also common for women to work underground here, engaged in the punishing work of bringing coals to the surface up a succession of ladders, in creels strapped to their backs.

The remains of the steelworks are now

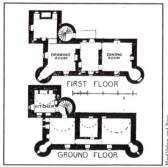

Monklands District Council

incorporated in a new park, set in the dramatic gorge of the North Calder Water to the east of the village.

The fluctuating fortunes of industry in Calderbank left a dismal social legacy. When the ironworks closed in 1888 most of its houses were boarded up and it took on the appearance of a deserted village. The 134 houses in Old and New Square (all now demolished) had to share eight dry privy middens located in the middle of the square as the focal point of their community. The Royal Commission on Housing visited Calderbank in 1914 and reported *So far as this and a large number of other conveniences in this county are concerned, the Public Health Acts might as well not exist.*

Calderbank Public School, Main Street, 1892, James Davidson
A simple rectangle with Gothic touches to reinforce the decorative gabled bargeboards and arched windows.

Calderbank Parish Church, Main Street, *c.*1860
Straightforward Gothic on a cruciform plan, ennobled by the square tower and transepts added by James Davidson in 1908, its belfry surmounted by octagonal pinnacles on each corner, seemingly out of touch with the more exciting architectural developments of its age.

Calderbank Police Station, Main Street, 1896, R Hamilton Paterson
A trio of pretty crowstepped gables to the road and a central broken pediment over its doorway. Too domestic in scale, however, to be a stern symbol of authority.

To the south-west of Calderbank lies the site of Woodhall House, the centrepiece of an estate acquired by Daniel Campbell of Shawfield, (1671-1753), the Glasgow merchant and MP for the Glasgow Burghs, who also purchased the island of Islay with government compensation received after the Shawfield Riots (see *Central Glasgow* in this series).

It was at **Faskine** that the *Vulcan* (*above & p.71*), the first iron-hulled passenger boat, was built in 1819, to the design of Sir John Robinson, for service on the Forth & Clyde Canal. With a length of 61 ft on a beam of 11 ft it was something of a marvel in its era and later saw service on the Clyde until 1873. A full-size replica is now on display at **Summerlee Heritage Museum** in **Coatbridge**. As steel foundries gradually replaced the ironworks, here the great hull plates for the *Queen Mary* were manufactured.

Below *Public School.*
Middle *Parish Church.*
Bottom *Police Station*

Peden

Peden

Peden

Monkland & Kirkintilloch Railway, was formed by an Act of 1824, opened in 1826, and ran from Palacecraig Colliery to the Forth & Clyde Canal basin at Kirkintilloch with horse-drawn wagons on a gauge of 4 ft 6 in. Shortly afterwards some of its subscribers experimented with wind propulsion and found that with a series of umbrella-shaped sails, the wagons could be conveyed successfully downwind. Needless to say the return journey posed some problems and the gentlemen had to resort to putting their shoulders to the task, agreeing, as they progressed, on the impracticability of this means of propulsion. The first steam engine was brought into use in 1831, designed by George Dodds and manufactured by Murdoch and Aitken – the first railway engine built in Glasgow. Branches were soon extended to Kipps and Rosehall, the company becoming the first empowered to carry passengers in Scotland.

University of Glasgow and Viscount Whitelaw

Woodhall House (*above & p.69*) was a splendid mansion by William Adam, the niched centrepiece similar to his (unbuilt) design for Elie House illustrated in *Vitruvius Scoticus*. Tragically Woodhall was burned out in the early years of this century and later demolished. Campbell's gardener at Woodhall was the skilled William Aiton, who subsequently laid out the Royal Gardens at Kew.

High Palacecraig, Sykeside Road, *c.1780* (*left*) A small, graceful white country villa lying to the west of Calderbank, three bays flanked by single-storey wings. It was once owned by the Whitelaw family who were active with the Bairds in ironfounding. It has a rear service courtyard. The contemporary replacement windows do it no favours and diminish its quality.

Monklands District Council

The first Scots railway, from Palacecraig to Kirkintilloch, opened less than a year after the more famous Stockton to Darlington line, and was steam hauled from 1831 by an early pair of *iron horses*, a precursor to the amazing proliferation of railways which would later serve the pits and ironworks throughout the Monklands and earn Coatbridge the epithet of the *Crewe of the North*.

Illustration of the first locomotive made in Glasgow in 1831 for the Monkland & Kirkintilloch Railway

Monklands District Council

COATBRIDGE

A true child of the Industrial Revolution, there is little pre-history to Coatbridge: until the 19th century, merely the *cottbrig*, a small bridge on the Colts estate, carrying the Airdrie to Glasgow road over the Gartsherrie Burn. The area was destined to undergo a most extraordinary transformation from rural backwater to the eighth largest town in Scotland in under a century. It became the famed *Iron Burgh* earning its own place in the history of world commerce.

The Statistical Account of 1799 describes the area effusively: *A great part of the Parish is enclosed, the advantages of which are universally allowed. Beside a vast quantity of natural wood, there are more than 1,000 acres planted. This beautifies the country and improves the climate. We have many extensive orchards, which some years turn out a great advantage. A stranger is struck with this view of the Parish. It has the appearance of an immense garden. Here are produced luxuriant crops of every grain, especially of wheat. The rivers abound with salmon in the proper season and trout of every species. There is also plenty pike and perch in the Monkland Canal and in the great lochs at the North side of the Parish, and taking of which, from small boats made for the purpose, is a pleasant amusement.* By the time of the Second Statistical Account in 1843, the immense garden was history. The invention in 1828 of the hot-blast process of ironsmelting by J B Neilson, an engineer at the Glasgow Gas Works, meant that the rich

Contemporary commentators were impressed: *There is no worse place out of Hell than that neighbourhood. At night, the groups of blast furnaces on all sides might be imagined to be blazing volcanoes at most of which smelting is continued on Sundays and weekdays, day and night, without intermission. From the town comes a continual row of the mass of heavy machinery: this and the pounding of many steam hammers seemed to make even the very ground vibrate under one's feet. Fire, smoke and soot with the roar and rattle of machinery are its leading characteristics; the flames of its furnaces cast on the midnight sky a glow as if of some vast conflagration. Dense clouds of black smoke roll over it incessantly and impart to all the buildings a peculiarly dingy aspect.*

Calder Tube Works

RCAHMS

Gartsherrie Iron & Coal Works

ironstone deposits of the Monklands could be exploited economically and the canal, originally *a measure for securing to the inhabitants of Glasgow at all times a plentiful supply of coal*, fortuitously provided the necessary means of distribution of the resulting iron products.

The environmental impact of the unfettered development of the *iron heart* of Coatbridge was stunning in its awfulness. The canal banks from Woodside to Coatdyke became a continuous procession of ironworks and were lined with no less than 160 puddling furnaces. Besides these were the workers' rows: terraces of cramped, single-end, tied houses, thrown up by the iron and coal masters as close as possible to the mine or ironworks. Tuberculosis was rife, but consolation from the ironmasters' Hades was provided by the sudden spate of church building.

Before a century had expired, the wheel of industrial technology had turned full circle: the blast-furnaces were cold and the revolution which had brought both prosperity and pollution left Coatbridge only the latter, along with a legacy of unemployment, appalling public housing conditions and some of the worst overcrowding in Scotland. It has taken several generations more for the Iron Burgh to exorcise this grimy ghost and to begin to rediscover the extraordinary heritage of its iron age.

Thomas Smith (1862-1941) was educated at Rosehall Works School and Gartsherrie Academy after his family moved to Coatbridge in 1871. Following architectural studies in Glasgow, he became a tutor at Glasgow School of Art, where in the mid 1880s, the young Charles Rennie Mackintosh was one of the evening pupils at his drawing class. Smith began in business on his own account in Coatbridge in 1887, being successful in obtaining commissions for a number of local churches – Blairhill, Cliftonhill Parish and Coatbridge Baptist Church amongst them. His civic role included the design of a number of Coatbridge Corporation housing schemes and he carried out a variety of commissions for Stewart & Lloyd, the Coatdyke iron masters. Entering public life in 1895 as a member of Old Monkland Parish Council, he became a Magistrate, Police Judge and eventually Provost of Coatbridge for a term of three years, his service being rewarded finally with appointment as Deputy Lieutenant of the County.

COATBRIDGE: Central
Baird Town
Coatbridge was built on seven hills, and by seven brothers Baird, who formed William Baird & Company. Born at **High Cross Farm** (near the Old Monkland Kirk), they found their way into iron production via coal mining and

by the latter part of the 19th century their
sixteen furnaces at Gartsherrie were Scotland's
leading producers of iron, holding a significant
share of world production. Having purchased
ground from the Colt family, they developed
Dunbeth Hill, laying out **Academy Street**,
Church Street, **St John's Street** and (of
course) **Baird Street**, determining feu
conditions and building. Idyllic cottages and
fine villas followed, most of which remain, with
a church and a school, all with the ashlar
frontages required by the feu. Comparison
with their workers' insanitary, overcrowded,
disease-ridden dwellings in the infamous
Gartsherrie Rows is extreme and unavoidable.
Baird Town, looking from its eminence over
towards the Gartsherrie furnaces and the
ironworkers' hovels, became a metaphor for
the new industrialism and its society.

Gartsherrie Church

Victorian photograph of Baird Street

1 **Gartsherrie Church**, Baird Street, 1839,
Scott Stephen & Gale (see p.72)
One of Coatbridge's first buildings, placed
immodestly at the apex of the hill to complete
the axes of **Baird Street** and **Church Street**,
Baird Street itself being aligned on the distant
vista of **Drumpellier House**. Slim red
sandstone spire like a Victorian Gothic
skyrocket aimed at immortality, being funded
mainly by the Bairds.

2 **Gartsherrie Academy**, Academy Street, 1845
(see p.52)
Designed to dominate the skyline with the
church and built by the Bairds for the children
of their workers at a cost of £2,500. Originally
it housed four separate schools with a total of
631 pupils. An unusually distinguished temple
design with a pedimented bay centrepiece very
reminiscent of the massing Alexander Thomson
was to make his leitmotif (see *Central Glasgow*
in this series) with fine scrolled brackets

Gartsherrie Academy

supporting the upper entablature and cupola. Original proportions somewhat disguised by later upper storeys: ominously boarded up.

3 **Carnegie Library**, Academy Street, 1905, Alexander Cullen (*below*)
A competition-winning design: two sandstone storeys of bold Renaissance design, swagged shields in the wings, and the town's arms over the entrance which welcomes the visitors positively in-between original Glasgow Style ironwork. Bookstacks to the rear have barrel-vaulted ceilings with beams on extended, sinuously curved corbels. Cullen here dabbled with the Mackintosh spirit that he was later to imbibe so enthusiastically. Andrew Carnegie provided £15,000 towards the cost of construction.

McArthur

James Baird of Gartsherrie (1802-76) (*above*) fourth son of Alexander Baird, took over active management of Baird & Co in 1830, just after the founding of Gartsherrie Iron Works. His talent for innovation and astute investment in new machinery had quadrupled output and over the next three decades he expanded the company throughout Central Scotland and as far afield as Cumberland, running up to fifty blast furnaces at their various works with an output of 300,000 tons of iron per annum and a labour force of over 10,000 men and boys. James paused only briefly to become Conservative MP for the Falkirk burghs in 1851-2 and like many other Victorian industrialists became increasingly absorbed in the acquisition of great estates both temporal and spiritual, becoming at once a substantial landowner and also one of the great benefactors of the Church of Scotland.

In 1873 he made the staggering gift of £500,000 to the Church *for the aid of struggling congregations* and followed this with the endowment of five new parish churches in Aberdeenshire and later of no less than 200 new parish churches in other parts of Scotland.

Monklands District Council

Academy Street, which runs down to **Main Street**, retains some elegance along the east side with a procession of civilised if unremarkable stone villas of the 1850s.
No 12-14, a later infill of 1890 by McLachlan for the National Bank, has red ashlar Ionic pilasters and stables to the rear.

The steep gradients of the streets in the Baird Town, following the natural contours of the hillside, were to prove a test to which many a horse and cart were unequal in Victorian times – loads having to be hauled up by a circuitous route rather than tackle the incline at Church Street.

Church Street was aligned to Gartsherrie Church from each side of the hill, both sections lined with well-mannered bijou stone cottages and villas for the petit bourgeoisie, those

fronting the church designed on an L-plan to emphasise the attempt at formal planning. **St John Street** is similarly laid out. **Lincoln Cottage**, No 60 St John Street, is a villa of the 1850s, the columned entrance with a central gablet over a shrine-like oriel window, retaining the original etched and painted, curved glazing. **Ashlea**, No 27, is distinguished by incised Greek ornament.

St John's Episcopal Church,
St John Street, 1843, G A O'Donoghue
A small Gothic church built to serve English ironworkers who flooded into Coatbridge to train local novices, refronted in ashlar by J H O'Donoghue in 1871, the buttresses with unusual colonettes in cast iron bearing foliated capitals. Chancel window by Adam & Small, 1881, the three-light west window (and others) by W & J J Keir, 1879. Threatened with demolition.

Bank of Scotland, Church Street, c.1900
Opulent Edwardian Jacobean in fine red sandstone, designed possibly by J M Arthur who produced a similarly asymmetrical design for the Bank in Airdrie in 1901.

Main Street
The famous bridges of Coatbridge are at the west end of Main Street where roads, railways, footpaths and canal all converge, a small vestige of the canal here now transformed into a pleasant landscaped area (see p.72).

4 **Airdrie Savings Bank**, Main Street, 1920, James Davidson (see p.72)
Corner block of three storeys in classic salmon-pink ashlar, the ground floor rusticated on a pink granite base. Tuscan columns at the splayed entrance, giant pilasters above with a

Top Church Street. *Middle top* Academy Street. *Middle bottom* 60 St John Street. *Above* Bank of Scotland, Church Street

Top *Airdrie Savings Bank.*
Top right *Victorian photograph of Royal Hotel.*
Above right *Victorian photograph of the Bridges.*
Above *Whitelaw Fountain*

balustrade and elongated convex dome.
Edwardian opulence just scraping into the
inter-war period.

5 **Whitelaw Fountain**, Main Street, 1875, Hugh
H McLure (see p.51)
Formerly in front of the Royal Hotel but, after
brushes with local traffic, at the gushet with the
South Circular Road. A sandstone and
polished granite confection on a rusticated base,
under an urned cupola dedicated to Alexander
Whitelaw, a partner in Gartsherrie Iron who, in
1872, organised the relocation of the railway
line away from Main Street at that point.

Shunters' Lounge, Sunnyside Road
Pretty little Victorian bar with a central
corbelled bay over Ionic pilasters, original little
turret and decorative slatework.

Main Street has since been pedestrianised, but
between 1974 and 1980 its south side suffered
dubious comprehensive redevelopment, its
legacy an amorphous shopping complex in alien
brickwork, addressed accusingly by the 19th-
century frontages on the other side of the street.

Coia's Central Café Ltd, Main Street, *c.*1928,
Thomas Smith
Four narrow storeys stand proud of their
neighbours like an émigré from an Amsterdam

Main Street

terrace, the decorative brick gable a reference to Smith's earlier Stewart & Lloyd offices.

6 **St Patrick's Church**, Main Street, 1896, Pugin & Pugin
This corner of St John Street has the finely composed gable frontage of St Patrick's, the star of Main Street, built on a site donated by the Bairds. Designed in Puginian Gothic in white Auchinlea sandstone, this Roman Catholic church was built for the thousands of Irish labourers and dispossessed Highlanders who flocked to Coatbridge to find work.

Above *St Patrick's Church.*
Left *Original competition drawing for Coatbridge Clinic by Alex Davidson*

7 **Public Baths & Clinic**, Main Street, 1938, Alexander Davidson
Competition-winning scheme in the stripped Scandinavian modernism of the late 1930s – forming a frigid courtyard. The pioneering combination of clinic and baths was a laudable attempt to improve the town's poor public health record of the era.

The courtyard, now in dire need of some sympathetic landscaping, sports a fine cubist (nude) sculpture by George B Innes.

Ellis Street
8 **Lanarkshire Coalmasters' Rescue Station**, 1914, James Davidson
Fine curved frontage reminiscent of railway architecture in the red smooth-faced brickwork finished with red sandstone dressings, arched windows and the name proudly displayed in a central pediment. The corner has a small bartizan for picturesque effect. Renovated as the **Fountain Business Centre** by William Nimmo & Partners in 1991.

9 **Cinema & Bingo Hall**, Ellis Street, 1936, McNair & Elder
A big brick box by Scotland's most prolific cinema architects, retaining some of its art

James Davidson (1848-1923), (*see p.70*) the son of a much-respected Airdrie weaver, began his working life as an apprentice joiner, attending technical classes in Glasgow to study building construction. While acting as foreman joiner on Flowerhill Parish Church in 1875, he was made Master of Works by the Baird Trust for a number of new church projects. Shortly afterwards he began practice as an architect in Coatbridge. He later became a councillor, magistrate and was elected Provost during 1909-12. His architectural work includes a number of schools and new bank buildings as well as theatres, including the King's Theatre in Edinburgh. His son Alexander (1880-1976) continued the practice, which is still active in Coatbridge.

Conditions in the works were primitive and perilous. At the puddling furnaces that lined the south side of Main Street, the highly skilled puddlers worked in intense heat, till they could literally pour the sweat out of their boots, and were only saved from dehydration by the expedient of sending the apprentice across the road for a pint (or more). They remained perfectly sober, otherwise they could not have survived at their dangerous trade.
Revd T Jardine Johnstone, Coatbridge Centenary Service, 1985

Top *Ellis Street cinema.*
Above *Department of*
Employment offices.
Right & below *Municipal*
Buildings

deco ornament on the entrance front where the exterior roughcast contrasts with red brick parapets.

10 **Department of Employment Offices**,
South Circular Road, 1988,
Hugh Martin & Partners
Long two-storey block, the ground floor and wings in red brickwork with V-shaped buttresses, the upper floor clad in greenish metal panels. Since at one time, having a Department of Employment at Coatbridge would have been pure Newspeak, this building has the air of an Orwellian Ministry of Culture.

DUNBETH

11 **Municipal Buildings**, Dunbeth Road, 1894,
A McGregor Mitchell (see p.51)
Solid civic virtue in pink Dumfries sandstone, originally focused on its vigorous pedimented, orielled and porticoed entrance bay, replete with swags and statues which was destroyed by fire and removed in 1967. The surviving bays fronting on Dunbeth Road were cut off in mid-pediment, so to speak. What remains is impressive enough: almost symmetrical palace front with stringcourse parapet and long pedimented windows focused upon two projecting bays with enormous pediments surging above the roofline, the southern flanked by niched statues of **Justice** by Ewing of Glasgow and **Industry** (Vulcan) by James Young striking heroic poses. Opulent Victorian interior. Presently being extended although a hard act to follow.

Muiryhall Street & Dunbeth
Road from east (demolished)

12 **Coatbridge High School**, Albert Street,
1908, H & D Barclay (see p.73)
The *Old Monkland School Board Higher Grade*
School given a worthy symmetrical frontage in red sandstone by the designers of Glasgow Academy. Each bay is defined by a heavily

rusticated buttress which supports an Ionic
column rising to the parapet. A weak central
pediment over surmounts the bold entrance.
The spirit of the age is only glimpsed in fine
Glasgow Style railings and, on each wing, the
familiar indented motif of four squares within
a square normally associated with Mackintosh.
Fine period **gymnasium** to the rear.

13 **Dunbeth Parish Church**, Weir Street, 1872,
Robert Baldie
Clearly the smart church of the town, towering
above the High School in Decorated Gothic. Its
sandstone, now a satanic black, serves only to
accentuate the height of the great octagonal
spire with its twelve pinnacles.

14 **Former Coatbridge Technical College**,
Kildonan Street, 1890, James Davidson
One of the world's first Technical Colleges,
built when Coatbridge was still in the
vanguard of technology in heavy industry,
although technically just a *School of Science
and Art*. Its fine pink sandstone façade is busy
with niches and pilasters, while the figures of
Science and **Art** recline in twin pediments
beside a fine urned balustrade. Too interesting
to be left neglected.

The Lodge House, Muiryhall Street, 1898,
Hugh McLure
A Baronial cottage orné behind the Council
Offices, packed with delights: shaped gables,
twin-finialed semi-dormers, a central
anthemion-capped oculus, Gothic chimney
stacks and more; originally the janitor's house
for Coatbridge High School, an imposing
château which stood to the east of the Lodge,
razed by fire in 1929. Its barrack-like
successors stand in dreary line abreast down

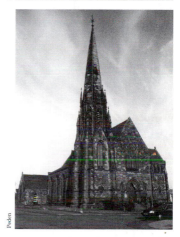

Top *Coatbridge High School.*
Middle *Dunbeth Parish Church.*
Above *Lodge House.*
Left *Muiryhall*

15 Muiryhall, the two great grey moderne blocks by J S Stewart in 1931 and 1934. A foil is provided by the surprisingly popular **Jackson 16 Flats** opposite, three multi-storey blocks of Scandinavian design from the early 1960s. From the west these merge together to form a seemingly massive rampart, whose height almost steals the thunder of the adjacent **Coats Church**.

Top *Jackson Flats*.
Above *Coats Parish Church*

17 Coats Parish Church, Jackson Street, 1874, Hugh McLure
Built with money left by George Baird, this idiosyncratic and picturesque buff sandstone landmark at the apex of Dunbeth Hill is dominated by its striking clock tower. The square, buttressed tower gives way to an octagonal lantern crowned with fleur-de-lys and pinnacles, inspired probably by the tower of the Cloth Hall at Bruges. From the bottom of the slope it seems pure Fonthill fantasy. The galleried interior contains a four-light window designed by Sir Edward Burne-Jones for William Morris's Studios. On a clear day the tower can be seen 20 miles away from Bridge of Allan.

DUNBETH

The affluent Victorian middle class claimed the physical (if not the moral) high ground at the summit of Dunbeth drumlin with a series of substantial villas. **Willesden** and **Derwent**, Laird Street, comprise an Italianate paired villa, 1890, fronted by a pair of two-storey bays under a pigeon-defying shark-toothed ridge.

Below *Willesden & Derwent*.
Bottom *Sunnyside Station*

18 Redholme, by Thomas Smith, adjacent, now the **Monklands Planning Department Office**, retains a few splendid Glasgow Style architraves and panelled doors (probably by Wylie & Lochhead).

   Belmont, Dunbeth Avenue, is an extensive villa with Arts & Crafts touches, the frontage set with decorated pilasters and with much turn-of-the-century leaded glass.

19 Sunnyside Station, Gartsherrie Road, 1888, Carswell (Architect to North British Railway)
Typical small single-storey halt, red brick with dressings in buff sandstone and contrasting yellow brick, with cast-iron columns with acanthus capitals supporting a big glazed canopy over the platform. Deserves to be sensitively refurbished.

20 **Lamberton Works**, Russell Colt Street, 1883
Giant red brick shed, relic of a Victorian heavy
engineering works, which survives in a
dramatic setting beside Summerlee. Its
business (Lamberton Robotics Ltd) defies the
demise of local engineering industries by
developing the manufacture of high-technology
robots for manufacturing processes.

21 **Greenhill Primary School**,
Coltswood Road, 1902, James Davidson
Set beside a little enclave of turn-of-the-
century villas in Inveresk Place, the school is
an unusual Renaissance composition in red
sandstone – shaped gables, urned parapets,
odd oval windows over the entrance doors –
which retains its entire ensemble of boundary
walls, railings and gates.

SUMMERLEE

22 **Summerlee Heritage Park**, 1988,
Monklands District Council Architects
A vivid display of the astonishing heritage of
the area. Factory buildings have been
renovated to form a spacious Machine
Exhibition Hall with a dramatic fully glazed
eastern gable, whilst the original works offices
of the 1830s have been refurbished as a visitor
centre and gallery. The frontage of another
Victorian engineering office now acts as
tearoom, and further transplants of industrial
architecture are planned. A section of the
Gartsherrie, **Hornock & Summerlee** branch
canal has been restored beside the **Howes
Basin**, which was used for transhipping coal
from the railway to the canal. Splendid
machine exhibits, working trams, steam
engines and a huge model of Summerlee
Ironworks in the 1880s. Not to be missed
(see pp.50, 68, 71). *Open to the public, entrance
free.* The works gatehouse survives on the east
of the access to Summerlee in sad disuse.

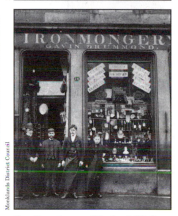

Top *Lamberton Works.* Middle
Greenhill Primary School.
Above *Victorian photograph of
Sunnyside.* Left *Summerlee
Heritage Park*

***The workers, too**, had their
pride in, and loyalty to, the
community, although their
condition was what we should
now judge as abject poverty. I
can remember a row of 'single
ends' – one roomed cottages – in
Sunnyside Road. Each had one
door and one window: and on
the door was an embossed metal
label proclaiming NOT MORE
THAN 4½ ADULTS. That
meant the couple in one box bed,
two weans in the other and a
baby in the cradle. Woe betide
them if there were more arrows
in the quiver. Revd T Jardine
Johnstone Coatbridge
Centenary Service, 1985*

Summerlee Ironworks
The Ironworks which Baird Town was built to overlook, opened in 1836 and eventually ran eight blast furnaces for almost a century, until its closure in 1930. Recently excavated from under 6m of later slag and industrial waste, its archaeological remains now serve **Summerlee Heritage Park**.

23 **Pullmans**, West Canal Street, 1899, George Graham
The former Central Station, very Arts & Crafty in smooth red brickwork with red sandstone dressings, overshot eaves and big arched openings on the ground floor. Its smart restaurant exterior contrasts with nearby Ross Street.

24 **Ross Street Hall**, Ross Street, 1898, James Davidson
Distinctive red sandstone corner block looking out over the canal, built as Masonic Hall and restaurant. Italianate first-floor windows and Corinthian pilasters boldly applied above a rusticated base.
    West Canal Street runs west from the bridges, the canal now culverted underground in a linear strip of landscape.

25 **Coatbridge Market**, Carradale Street, 1896, A McGregor Mitchell (see p.70)
Picturesque livestock market – a fine red brick shed with the massive carved head of a bull projecting from its south-facing Dutch gable — entered beneath a broken pediment. Truncated roof. Entrance pillars and **lodge** on **West Canal Street** overwhelmed by later huts. Now

Top Summerlee Iron Works. Middle Pullmans. Above Ross Street Hall. Right Coatbridge Market

The Bairds amassed enormous wealth and, in the best traditions of Victorian industrialists, used this to purchase estates and thereby a position in landed society. Later scions of the family were less prudent with this legacy. **Abingdon Baird**, a suitor of Lily Langtry, became notorious at the turn of the century for his escapades of glorious profligacy, his infatuation with slow horses and fast women assisting him in parting with his inheritance at the rate of half a million pounds a year. He died in debt, but with 86 racehorses in his stables.

Top *Anderson Street, Airdrie.*
Left *Covenanting gravestone at
Kirk o' Shotts.* Middle *Cairnhill
Doocot.* Above *Arran View*

Top *Black Bull, Airdrie.*
Above *Bank of Scotland,
Airdrie.* Top right *Summerlee
Heritage Park.* Right *Kirk o'
Shotts.* Below *Monklands
Leisure Centre, Airdrie*

50

Top *Time Capsule, Coatbridge.*
Left *Whitelaw Fountain,*
Coatbridge. Middle *New Cross,*
Airdrie. Above *Municipal*
Buildings, Coatbridge

51

a Council depot. The adjacent red sandstone
gateway and ornamented iron gate lead to
26 **Coatbridge Bowling Club**, pretty Edwardian
of 1902 by Thomas Martin in red brick with
yellow quoins rather in the character of railway
architecture, which heralds **Bowling Street**, a
leafy area of late-Victorian red sandstone
villas: **Drumlea**, No 4, whose rear coachhouse
shelters a small doocot in the gable; **Kenmure**,
No 9, whose north wing is resplendent with
period leaded glass. **Bowling Street** once
backed directly on to an area of extreme
contrast – a square enclosure of ironworkers'
rows – named **Merryston Square**, after
James Merry MP, the Carnbroe ironmaster.

The fine prettily balustraded iron bridge over
the canal at the foot of Blairhill Street here
27 also bears his name, **Merryston Bridge**, and
retains the pillars for its original gas lighting.

Monkland Canal

The high prices and trade monopoly of Glasgow
coal merchants in the mid-18th century
prompted the construction of the Monkland
Canal, as a means of transport for the
Monklands colliers in carting their product to
Glasgow. Retained by James Buchanan to
survey and report on a suitable route, James
Watt produced two schemes, with and without
locks: the latter – a cheaper but more
meandering canal – was chosen. Work started
in 1770, with Watt supervising the Irish
navigators (or *navvies* as they became known),
the supply of water for the early section being
obtained by forming a new reservoir at
Drumpellier Moss which at the time was the
largest man-made reservoir in the world.
Funds ran out in 1773 following the liquidation
of the Ayr Bank, after the completion of only
the first seven miles, from Sheepford to
Blackhill. Business on this restricted length of
waterway was at first slow, the outward-bound
coal barges from Dundyvan, Coats and
Drumpellier being returned with the two
available means of organically enriching the
soil, lime and human manure from the privies
of Glasgow. In 1790, the canal was bought by
Stirling of Drumpellier, a coal owner, and by
William Stirling & Company, coal merchants
who pushed eastwards to Faskine and
Calderbank. It was nearly forty years later
that the coal canal was exploited to its full
extent, when the ironworks began to appear all
along its banks at Coatbridge and Airdrie.

Coatbridge, c. 1855

A hunner funnels bleezin',
reekin',
Coal an' ironstane charrin',
smeekin',
Navvies, miners, keepers, fillers,
Puddlers, rollers, iron millers;
Reestit, reekit, ragged laddies,
Firemen, enginemen an'
Paddies;

Thick and thrang we see them
gaun
First the dram shop, then the
pawn;
Oure a' kin's o' ruination
Drink's the King in our location.

from *Oor Location*, Janet
Hamilton of Coatbridge
(1795-1873)

Opposite: Top left *Flowerhill
Parish Church, Airdrie.* Middle
left *Gartsherrie Academy,
Coatbridge.* Right *Old College
gateway, Airdrie.* Bottom
Stanley House

D

Andrew Stewart Fountain

Holy Trinity & All Saints

Alexander McGregor Mitchell (1842-1904) spent his early years on Rosehall Estate, where his father was factor and later was schooled at Dundyvan Academy. His earliest architectural appointment was in connection with the Deaf and Dumb Institute in Glasgow, later he worked for William Shanks, an architect in Airdrie. Opening his own practice, Mitchell became Master of Works to the Buchanans of Drumpellier and architect to the Colts of Gartsherrie, following this with the appointment as Coatbridge Burgh Engineer. He was known as one of the *men who built the town* in Coatbridge and the Municipal Buildings remain as his principal work, in addition to major sections of Coathill Fever Hospital, Coatdyke Parish Church and a number of schools throughout the county.

Ironically, it was Watt's own invention, the steam engine, which sounded the canal's eventual death knell in the form of railway transport. In the mid 1960s it was officially closed, culverted underground between Sikeside and Blair Road. Remaining stretches are now being redeveloped as an historic and recreational asset, and an extensive town and country walkway has been formed along its towpaths. There are plans to re-open further sections for passenger traffic.

COATBRIDGE: East COATDYKE

28 **Holy Trinity & All Saints** and **Manse**, Muiryhall Street East, 1904, A McGregor Mitchell
An Edwardian decorated shed, impressive in scale, heavily buttressed in Gothic red sandstone, the raised site emphasising its tall four-pinnacled tower. The attached church hall was built five years later in matching materials and adds considerably to the composition.

29 **Andrew Stewart Fountain**, Muiryhall Street East, 1888, J C Jamieson (Crown Granite Works, Aberdeen)
Modestly scaled memorial in polished granite erected to celebrate Coatbridge becoming a burgh (three years earlier) by A J Stewart, the ironfounder, on the site of Coatdyke Cross, once the centre of the iron village of Coatdyke or Cowdyke which merged into Coatbridge in the mid 19th century.

30 **Monklands District Court**, Main Street, 1906, Thomas Smith (see p.71)
Thumping magisterial authority, built originally as Stewart & Lloyd's offices (note the legend SSL set out in contrasting colours of brick). The court building has a striped brick plinth with four round-arched windows and an

Monklands District Council

almost entirely glazed upper storey. The three-bay centrepiece is identified by a round-arched pediment.

Andrew J Stewart moved his ironfounding business to Coatbridge in the 1860s, his Clyde Tube Works being built in 1865 (the move from Glasgow reputedly being prompted by Coatbridge's notorious tolerance of environmental pollution). The company expanded to become the largest tube manufacturers

RCAHMS

31 **Coatdyke Parish Church**, Muiryhall Street, 1897, T Smith
A simple grey sandstone Gothic ensemble with token belltower, partly endowed by Stewart & Lloyd thus earning it the name of the *Iron Church*. To the north are the housing estates of **Cliftonville** by A McGregor Mitchell, named after the Tobacco Lord who owned Moorihall House in the early 19th century, dubbing it Cliftonhill after his native Bristol.
Cliftonville, the first estate of *homes for heroes* built by Coatbridge Council after the First World War, consists of well-built two-storey cottages laid out in garden-city style in two phases after Parker & Unwin by Alex

in Great Britain, its Sun Foundry and Tube Works being opened in 1884, the British Tube Works in Dundyvan Road five years later, and the largest, the Imperial Tube Works in 1900. At the Imperial, tubing of all sizes, from one-eighth of an inch to 6 ft in diameter was once manufactured. The area around Coatdyke thus became known as *Stewart's Land*. The dramatic departure of the tube manufacturing plant to Corby in 1934 was felt to presage the decline of Scottish heavy industry. The Clyde Tube Works was later converted to a whisky bond.

Top *Coatbridge Workshops.*
Above *Deedes Street corner*

Coatbridge Rows at South Burn Road by George Arthur, 1903. These room-and-kitchen houses were more generously proportioned than the earlier rows, but even here one of the houses shows accommodation for two adults and an unspecified number of children in a total floor area of 15 ft 6 in. by 17 ft. Note the box beds in the kitchens

McGregor Mitchell Jnr in 1922 and 1933. This spacious and attractive development is focused

32 on its little green at **Agnew Avenue**. Few later municipal housing schemes shared the same success.

Coatbridge Business Centre, Main Street, James Davidson & Son
Boringly businesslike, the blue metal roof and green trim confirm a thorough modernity.

33 **Coatbridge Workshops**, Coatbank Street, 1990, Thomson McCrae & Sanders, have risen from the ashes of the Phoenix Iron Works beside what was once the canal. A sweeping courtyard in buff bricks with a beige metal roof, the apex barrel-vaulted in red-framed glazing thus echoing the nearby **Victoria Estate**.

34 **Deedes Street**
The corner with **Rochsolloch Road**, J M Arthur, is turned by the ogee-capped tower of a distinctive Glasgow Style commercial corner block built for Robert Chapman in 1899, with a spiky skyline. Only one pair of its original arched display windows survives. **South Burn**

35 **Road** and **Railway Road** by J M Arthur, 1896 onwards, opposite, retain the last remnants of the Coatbridge rows, most of which were systematically cleared by the early 1960s: a double row of tiny back-to-back single-ends (now converted to workshops). The amazingly cramped pattern of occupation in these brick hutches can be seen by the original house numbers over the doors.

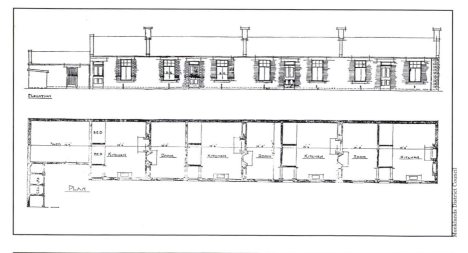

COATBRIDGE : South
WHIFFLET

Known as Wheatflat in the mid 17th century, suggesting that the monks used these flat-lands south of the Luggie Burn for cereal. It was to be rendered unrecognisable by the ironmasters with a solid mass of engineering workshops, foundries and railways.

36 **Whifflet Foundry**, Tennant Street
The last reminder of the scale of that vigorous industrial development: a procession of cyclopean red brick sheds, the entrance on Whifflet Street in contrasting 1930s style with glass block panels, the gable of its offices curved, dynamically vertical windows and capped by a once-heroic flagpole. Adjacent **Calder Works** have been cleared by British Steel, leaving dereliction.

Whifflet Street presents the opposing images which characterise much of this post-industrial landscape. Pleasant turn-of-the-century façades on the west (including 1909 shops and flats by Thomas Martin) surveying the tired-looking 1970s **shopping centre** and desperately drab high flats on the east by T N Smith. These replaced the infamous Rosehall Rows, illustrations of which were used by George Orwell in *The Road to Wigan Pier* to depict the privations suffered by the working class. They were built by the ironmaster Robert Addie who leased the mineral rights from the Douglas Support estate in 1837, and built Langloan ironworks four years later.

37 **Garturk Parish Church**, Calder Street, 1870, Hugh H McLure (*right*)
A substantial piece of blond sandstone Gothic, rose window gable to the street, entrance beneath the square tower whose four pinnacles flank a tall, lucarned octagonal spire. Attached **manse** at the rear. Its resemblance to a kirk for douce bourgeoisie conceals the fact that its early congregation came from the rather different background of the Whifflet miners' rows.

BARROWFIELD
38 **St Mary's**, Hozier Street, 1896, Pugin & Pugin, is a standard twin-aisled Gothic kirk in blond sandstone; pretty and extensive **presbytery** attached. The construction was

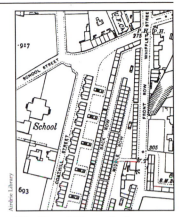

Airdrie Library

The Royal Commission on the Housing of the Working Classes of Scotland, which visited the Rows (*above*) in March 1914 reported: *They consist of four long parallel rows of single-storey hovels. Most of them have no rones to carry the rainwater from the roof. Rainfall simply runs down the roof and then runs down the walls or falls down by chance as the wind decides. Coals are kept below the beds. The closet accommodation is hideous. A number of these hovels are built back to back. The closets outside are not used by the women. In some of the rows 7 or 8 people occupy a single room. The sanitary conveniences were in a state of revolting filth. They* were eventually cleared in the 1920s and replaced by the current housing between Coathill Street and Whifflet Street.

Peden

Top *St Mary's Church.*
Above *Barnyard Inn.*
Right *Coathill Hospital*

supervised by A McGregor Mitchell. Thomas
39 Baird's grim **Primary School**, 1909, perhaps
reflects that education at that date may have
been just as unforgiving as the grey
authoritarian elevations suggest. Alex
Davidson's **Free Church**, 1936, in Hozier
Street is rather an economic model.
Wallace Street is terminated by the
40 **Barnyard Inn**, 1896, James Davidson,
originally adjacent to Whifflet Farm, a red
sandstone corner block typical of the era,
weighed down by a motley collection of
dormers.

41 **ROSEHALL**
Whifflet Public School, School Street, 1886,
James Higgins
A competition-winning design which doubtless
looked impressive enough when set in the
context of the Rosehall Rows. The inset
Tuscan-columned entrances are now largely
concealed by execrable later extensions.

42 **Coathill Hospital**, Hospital Street, 1861,
Robert Baird
The Old Monkland Poorhouse, founded to allow
the old, sick and unemployed to earn the
generosity of the Parish in its spartan
workhouse. The location of the Fever Hospital
on the same hillside in 1874 confirmed Coathill
as the last resort of the poor and the sick
throughout the area. The main 1874 block also
by Robert Baird is a plain red sandstone
barracks on a grand scale, advanced wings
implying a palace frontage without a
centrepiece. Single-storey ward blocks in
various forms by A McGregor Mitchell
followed, separated to avoid cross-infection.
The **Superintendent's house** and **lodge**,
1910, are also on a substantial scale, the house
in red sandstone with a suitably Edwardian
air, the half-timbered gables revealing a
southern influence.

SHAWHEAD

MSA Factory, Hagmill Road, 1984,
William Nimmo & Partners
Essay of elegance and some symmetry in dark brown metal cladding over buff brickwork which lies close to the spot on the North Calder Water where the Cistercians built the Hagg Mill to grind the corn of their Monklands. Further downstream lies the site of the now-vanished Douglas Support House – which Rosehall House became thus christened after its laird, Archibald Stewart, was supported by the Duchess of Douglas, in a gruelling legal action against the Duke of Hamilton.
Rosehall, with its stepped terraces, is a sad loss: a great house added to in the 17th, 18th and early 19th centuries without ever losing its majesty.

43 **Grange Hotel**, Kirkshaws Road, 1905,
Thomas Smith
A two-storey Edwardian double villa in buff sandstone has its share of Glasgow Style motifs and a prospect over the M8.

44 **Nos 250-254 Whifflet Street** is a terrace of single-storey houses of the mid 19th century; **No 246**, the manager's house for Rosehall Pits, a little cottage orné with decorative ironwork details and an anthemion capped, pedimented entrance, enlivens an avenue rank with uneven development and gap sites.

KIRKWOOD

45 **Old Monkland Parish Church & church hall**, Woodside Street, 1790
Just north of the site of the ancient medieval parish kirk (a tithe of one of the canons of Glasgow Cathedral) is a large red sandstone box kirk fronted by an entrance tower

The Douglas Cause
This extraordinary legal battle to decide the Douglas succession occupied the Scottish Law Lords for six years (1762-7), the action being between two claimants, the Duke of Hamilton and Archibald Stewart, who was financially supported by his aunt Margaret, Duchess of Douglas. The decision went against Stewart, the published decree and judgement running to 9,676 pages, but was reversed in 1769 on appeal to the House of Lords, declaring Stewart the heir to the vast Douglas estates. At this popular result, jubilant crowds in Edinburgh wreaked havoc on the houses of those Lords of Session who had voted adversely in the original action and the militia had to be called in to restore order. The Duchess re-named Rosehall estate *Douglas Support* after the victory, and its mansion became known as Douglas Support House.

Top *Douglas Support House.* Above *Grange Hotel.* Left *Old Monkland Parish Church*

reminiscent of the old steeple at Glenmavis. The lancet windows were originally divided below the oculi, those on the south wall were later joined for decorative effect. The enormous graveyard has many 18th- and 19th-century monuments of interest, and a few earlier stones. Formerly it housed the Egyptian tomb of the Douglas family.

46 **Kirkstyle Cottages**, Kirkshaws Road, 1904, Thomas Smith
Two splendid pairs of Edwardian semi-detached villas in well-observed but idiosyncratically interpreted half-timbering, with jettied upper floors and lich-gate entrances. All are combined into a magisterial symmetry by slate roof with red clay focused upon a tall, central pavilion roof with a great brick chimney stack at the apex.

Top *Kirkstyle Cottages.*
Above *Mitchell Street*

47 **Mitchell Street**, 1947,
James Davidson & Partners
Excellent examples of post-war terraced houses, with an unusual vocabulary of mono-pitched roofs, bull's-eye and corner windows, brickwork eaves' details contrasting with roughcast walling, very much in the post-war Swedish mode, as built by Kininmonth & Spence in Forth. The elevated setting gives a fine prospect over the Drumpellier estate.

COATBRIDGE: West
BLAIRHILL
A plantation until the end of the 19th century when a burgeoning middle class sought to distance itself from the noisome collieries and iron works by retreating into substantial houses uphill. The large merchant villas of

Below *Lefroy Street.*
Bottom *Manor Park*

Lefroy Street (Lefroy being a maiden name of a member of the Buchanan family) take pride of place at the summit of the hill, the lower slopes reserved for lesser villas, semi-detached houses and terraces in descending order of social elevation. 48 **Manor Park**, *c.*1880, has a fine rooftop penthouse to survey industry and the proletariat from a safe distance. Most of the villas are Italianate (**Claremont**, 1881, decorated with Corinthian pilasters and a wonderful glass house on the lower floor) and all are set above the road for imposing effect, with fine views to the south. Many original coachhouses remain to the rear of the villas on **Muir Street**, the equine accommodation rather superior to the ironworkers' conditions in the Summerlee Rows a few hundred yards away. **Wood Street** leads down the hill towards **West End Park**, No 34 a Glasgow Style villa of red sandstone, frontage distinguished by balustered projecting bays and fine curved pediments.

49

Blairhill Street, a long leafy avenue which originally led up to Summerlee House, climbs up from Merryston Bridge. **Blairhill Parish Church** by T Smith, 1892, is red sandstone Gothic and surprisingly unadventurous for the tutor of Charles Rennie Mackintosh.

50

Above *Blairhill Church.*
Left *Kenilworth House*

Below *Wemyss Park.*
Bottom *Espieside*

51 **Kenilworth House**, the largest of Blairhill's piles, is an enormous, rather untidy, red brick Edwardian composition by A McGregor Mitchell with a Gothic flavour, now a nursing home. Turreted **North Park** sits behind its effusively decorative cast-iron gates; and at the
52 corner of Muir Street, **Wemyss Park** hints at Glasgow Style influence in its gabled composition.

53 **Espieside**, Blair Road, 1905
Boldly detailed delight of Edwardian Baronial in rustic dark-red sandstone under crowsteps.
54 Its contemporary, **Killygordon**, beside the hospital, is more consistently Glasgow Style in character.

55 **Alexander Hospital**, Blair Road, 1897,
A McGregor Mitchell
Endowed by John Alexander, first Provost of Coatbridge and partner in William Baird & Company, the crowstepped central block in restrained Baronial red sandstone is flanked by matching wings; much extended.

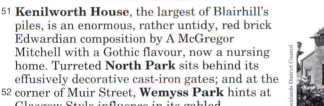

56 St Ambrose High School, Blair Road, 1972,
Alison Hutchison & Partners
Very large and very glazed in the fashion of the
time, with much cranked patent glazing on the
57 west front. New **games hall** added by
Strathclyde Regional Council Architects at the
rear (1990) in well-handled blockwork and
wriggly tin, in a curious interpretation of neo-
classicism.

Top *St Ambrose High School.*
Above *Coatbridge War
Memorial*

58 Coatbridge War Memorial, West End Park,
1927, Edith Burnet Hughes
Won in competition by Sir J J Burnet's niece,
one of the Glasgow Girls, this elegant open
drum of six granite columns round a central
urn sits in the corner of West End Park, which
was gifted to Coatbridge by the Buchanans.
The flats opposite are by T N Smith. The
59 Janet Hamilton Memorial, a competition-
winning design, 1880, by Petrie of Aberdeen, is
a poetically simple pillar surmounted by an urn
in pink and grey granite: originally a drinking
fountain erected in memory of the local bard
who had lived nearby in Langloan Cottages, its
opening ceremony was attended by an
estimated crowd of 20,000 who marched
through the town behind local bands to its
unveiling.

LANGLOAN
60 St Augustine's Church, Buchanan Street,
1907, Pugin & Pugin
A formidable red sandstone ensemble: twin-
aisled kirk in geometric Gothic with a huge
traceried window over an impressive triple
doorway. The **presbytery** with Tudor Gothic
windows is otherwise matching. A later hall
block in stylish Arts & Crafts.

St Augustine's Parish Church

61 Monklands Leisure Centre, Bank Street, 1977, Peter Womersley
Civic sports centre in a crisp geometric composition of panelled forms and angled patent glazing: offices on bridge-like battered supports, upper floors cantilevered out towards the road and the now subterranean canal. It demonstrates that carefully designed and detailed modernism could, in the hands of a master, be as architecturally distinguished as any other style. Not as energetically sculptural as much of Womersley's earlier work, and one of his last schemes in Britain.

Monklands Leisure Centre

Buchanan Street was named reputedly after Andrew Buchanan, blacksmith of Langloan Smithy which once flourished here. The leisure centre is dragged into the 21st century through
62 the addition of the **Time Capsule**, 1991, by Limbrick Grayshon Associates, an ingenious combination of leisure pool and ice rink. The entrance is designed in the back-to-the-future vernacular of Dan Dare and Flash Gordon, the interior under its ridge light dramatically structural, the jacuzzis a far cry from the tin baths in the Langloan miners' single-ends. Architecturally being little more than a long low shed, it is regressive when compared to the formal qualities of the Leisure Centre (see p.51).

Time Capsule

63 Dundyvan Church, Henderson Street, 1905, Alexander Cullen (see p.71)
Distinguished red sandstone church of the Scots revival, with some similarity to Sir J J Burnet's majestic Barony Kirk (see *Central Glasgow* in this series). The slim buttressed gable with etiolated lancet windows is reminiscent of a transept of Glasgow

Dundyvan Church

On the near bank of the Luggie once stood the Long Row: a spectacular terrace of tiny iron and coal workers' houses over a third of a mile long. It was built by John Wilson, the Dundyvan ironmaster, and interrupted only by Dundyvan No 5 coal mine which was sunk between two gable ends. Many of the houses lay within a stone's throw of the eight open-topped furnaces of Dundyvan Ironworks which were fired day and night, seven days a week. The houses boasted all the usual conveniences of such rows: no gas, dry outside toilets and water from a communal standpipe in the street.

Cathedral. The tall, pinnacled belfry tower, culminating in its splendid crown can, by virtue of its commanding site over the Luggie Burn, be seen for miles. Now worryingly vacant and unused. The attached **manse** is consummately Glasgow Style of the solid Scots massing of Mackintosh, with leaded glass of the period.

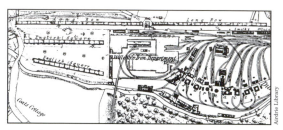

64 **Langloan Primary School**, Blair Road, 1914, James Davidson
Unusually substantial red sandstone school for the children of the Langloan Rows whose parents worked at Langloan Iron & Chemical Works or the nearby Drumpellier No 4 colliery. Plain elevations given elegance, pedimented pavilions and pinnacled urns, perched high on the parapets.

DRUMPELLIER
Drumpellier Park Visitor Centre, Townhead Road, 1984, Monklands District Council Architects
Elongated lodge, well detailed in buff brickwork and dominated by a wide-pitched fibre slate roofscape. Site lapped by the waters of **Lochend Loch**.

Drumpellier House, begun 1741, (demolished)

Top *Langloan Primary School*. Above *Drumpellier Park Visitor Centre*. Top right *Long Row, Dundyvan Ironworks*

Drumpellier House

The seat of Andrew Buchanan, a Glasgow Tobacco Lord who purchased the estate in 1735, transforming much of the policies into a landscaped pleasure ground, parkland in the manner of Capability Brown, a loch and a swanhouse. His descendant Carrick Buchanan generously gifted the estate to the town of Coatbridge in 1919, becoming a fine public country park and golf course. Buchanan's mansion was eventually demolished, its place being assumed by the present comparatively insubstantial golf clubhouse on Drumpellier Avenue.

When the loch was drained in 1931, the remains of an Iron Age crannog (fortified loch dwelling) of about *c.*100 BC were uncovered. Investigation revealed that it had been burnt down and rebuilt several times, finally being abandoned about AD 500. The two human skeletons uncovered seemed to suggest that the last inhabitants had died a violent death, probably at the hands of another invading tribe. The site is sometimes visible as a mound of stones at times of low water level.

Burial ground of the Buchanans

The Buchanans of Drumpellier

Andrew Buchanan (1690-1759), a descendant of John Buchanan, the *King of Kippen*, became one of Glasgow's immensely wealthy Virginia merchants and was swept up on the great tidal wave of tobacco trade prosperity to become Lord Provost of Glasgow in 1740. Buchanan Street remains named after him. The Drumpellier estate was purchased in 1735, but the fortunes of the family abruptly foundered when the American revolutionaries seized their Virginia plantations. Andrew's grandson, David Carrick Buchanan, later emigrated to Virginia and made his fortune, allowing him to repurchase Drumpellier. The Buchanans were no Jacobites; when Prince Charles sent them a letter demanding a £500 campaign contribution, on pain of the plunder of their house, Andrew Buchanan called his bluff: *Plunder awa' then– I'll no pay a single farthing.*

Drumpellier Doocot

65 The **Home Farm** (*above*), a happy survivor of the early 1820s, is an enormous square courtyard backing on to the Monkland Canal measuring nearly 100 yards on each side, containing byres, stables and wagon stores. It is laid out round a now ruined circular brick doocot, all constructed in weathered red sandstone, crowstepped and slated. The scale of the stables speaks volumes about the wealth of Buchanan's estate.

66 The **West Lodge**, Glasgow Road, 1826, is an elegant classical gatehouse with pedimented

The influx of skilled English pig-iron workers, which earned Coatbridge its sobriquet of the *Staffordshire of Scotland* also stimulated cricket in Scotland, the Buchanans becoming patrons of Drumpellier Cricket Club (founded 1850). In 1877 W G Grace travelled to Scotland with his United South of England team for a twenty-a-side match, but the iron men of Drumpellier routed Grace's team, who lost by 116 runs.

67 gables and a Doric-columned entrance, shamefully vandalised. The **Burial Ground** of the Buchanans moulders at the rear amongst trees beside Drumpellier golf course, which now occupies much of the Tobacco Lord's parks. 68 The contemporary **East Lodge**, Drumpellier Avenue, survives in similar classic form, its entrance advanced and arched, though suffering severely from later alterations. The lodges were built when the estate was enclosed with a high rubble wall to prevent the invasion of the grounds by the great numbers of immigrant labourers that the Coatbridge coal pits had begun to attract.

Right Drumpellier West Lodge. Below *Drumpark Special School*

Drumpark Special School, Coatbridge Road, 1926, J Stewart, Lanarkshire County Architect
Built on a butterfly plan more like a sanatorium than a school, focused upon a polygonal tower of the central block in red brick with sandstone dressings.

COATBRIDGE: West BARGEDDIE
With Cuilhill and Langmuir, Bargeddie formed a trio of mining hamlets to the west of Coatbridge which flourished in the early days of the coal canal, coals from Langmuir and Bargeddie being carried by rail to the loading wharf on the canal at Cuilhill Gullet, and thence to Glasgow. Bargeddie remained a village until the overwhelming arrival of council estates to house Glasgow overspill.

St Kevin's Church

St Kevin's Church, Rosebank Terrace, 1950, Gillespie, Kidd & Coia
One of a series of ten long-plan economic churches Coia designed immediately after the war, very different from the dynamic modelling

Davidson

— South Elevation —

which characterised his firm's later work, but derivative from the pre-war patterns. As usual, the quality lies within.

Bargeddie School & School House,
Coatbridge Road, 1894, James Davidson
Baronial with crowsteps, ball finials and toothed eaves: a pretty H-plan school in pink sandstone. Adjoining schoolhouse more effective on a smaller scale. Built to serve all three hamlets, Cuilhill and Langmuir have now disappeared with their pits and rows.

Drumpellier West Lodge,
Coatbridge Road, c.1880
Arched entrance with columns and foliated capitals, oculi, fretted bargeboards and a bracketed balcony under Italianate windows. Possibly the colliery manager's house for the Bartonshill pits around Cuilhill.

Bargeddie Parish Church, Manse Road, 1876, W & R S Ingram
Isolated from its village on the far side of the M8, this archaeological Gothic landmark stands in splendid isolation, its slim belfry and spire soaring to a tremendous elevation. Accomplished and complex, it has angled transepts and a baptistry, all in blushing pink sandstone. The site was originally gifted by the Misses Black of Heatheryknowe, one of whom received both her temporal and spiritual reward by later marrying the first minister. It cost £7,600 including manse and lodge.

COATBRIDGE: North GARTSHERRIE
Originally Gartsearraigh (or kail farm). With the neighbouring area of Townhead, this farming district was owned by the Colt family

Original drawing for Bargeddie School by James Davidson

It was in the Lochwood mine at Cuilhill, owned by the ubiquitous Bairds of Gartsherrie, that the first chain-driven coal-hewing machine in Scotland, known as the *Gartsherrie*, was introduced in 1864. Bargeddie was thus, albeit briefly, at the cutting edge of Victorian technology. Though plagued by unreliability at the time, this machine became the prototype for mechanical coal-hewing equipment into the 20th century.

Bargeddie Parish Church

Peden

who had settled in the locality when Ranulphus Le Colt was granted lands here by William the Lion in the 12th century. Their bridge over the Gartsherrie Burn bore the family name, inadvertently thus giving name to the village which was to grow up there in the early 19th century – Coatbridge – while the family became the Colts of Gartsherrie of that Ilk. Their seat, **Gartsherrie House**, now lies under the tarmac of the freightliner terminal, although its lodge still survives. In 1832, John Hamilton Colt sold the mineral rights of Gartsherrie to the Bairds for £34 15s 9d a year on a 999-year lease, somewhat naïvely one might think. Within 30 years the furnaces of the Gartsherrie Works were utilising 200,000 tons of iron ore and 100,000 tons of coal annually and the fame of Gartsherrie No 1 iron had rung round the globe. Gartsherrie Works, by far the largest in Coatbridge, outlived the other foundries, but eventually closed in 1967.

Gartsherrie House

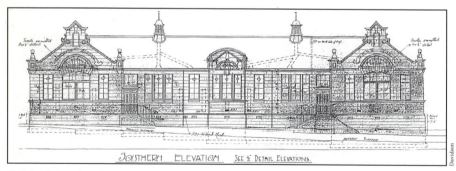

Original drawing for Gartsherrie School by James Davidson

69 **Gartsherrie Primary School**, Gartsherrie Road, 1906, J Davidson
Pleasant single-storey, red sandstone, school with vaguely Renaissance details in the wings and a central gablet.

Gartsherrie Holm Farm, Gartgill Road, 1872
Gothic villa in a rural setting which once housed the Colts' farm manager, their arms grandly emblazoned in the centre gable.

Coltswood House, Coltswood Road, c.1860
Substantial villa, originally known as Gartsherrie Cottage.

Opposite: Top Woodhall House. Middle left and below Summerlee Heritage Park. Middle right Woodville, Victoria Place, Airdrie. Bottom right Airdrie Academy

MILNCROFT
Milncroft Mill, Millcroft Road, c.1800
Picturesquely sited in the valley of the Shank Burn, a mile south of Greenfaulds, the internal overshot timber mill wheel of this former

Above *Provost James Davidson FRIBA*. Top right *Coatbridge Market*. Right *Caldercruix Parish Church*. Below *St Andrew's Hospice, Airdrie*. Bottom *British Steel Imperial Works, Rochsolloch*

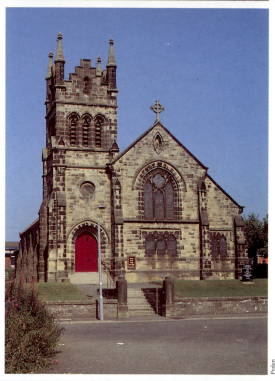

Left *Summerlee Heritage Park.*
Bottom left *New Monkland
Parish Church, Glenmavis.*
Below *Vulcan.* Middle
Monklands District Court.
Bottom *Dundyvan Church,
Coatbridge*

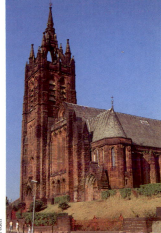

71

Peden

Peden

Peden

Peden

cornmill still exists along with the associated gearing and machinery. The mill lade once entered at upper level in the south-east corner of the Mill. Now converted as a house. The original miller's cottage is extant on the other side of Millcroft Road.

Milncroft Mill

CLEDDANS

Cleddans House, Condorrat Road, 1849
Smart white country house in magisterial Jacobean, somewhat in the style of William Burn, built for one McHardie, Sheriff-Clerk of Glasgow. Shaped gables and dormer finials vie with diamond-cut chimney stacks to provide a

Cleddans House

challenging skyline above knots of decorative strapwork ornament and buckle quoins, all built in a fine yellow ashlar and looking out over its walled garden. A brick arched tunnel links the rear to **Cleddans Stables** at the north. Contemporary **stables** form a U-shaped range of some character, though the horses had to make do with a simple Scots vernacular the barns and cartshed having crowstep gables over plain rubble walls, the east gable with a doocot inset. Now converted for domestic use, the main house a nursing home.

GLENBOIG

Lying to the north of Coatbridge, this industrial village sprang to life in the early 19th century, originally (and less decorously) known as Glenbog. It was almost a wholly owned estate of the world-renowned *Glenboig Union Fireclay Company. Famed in every country in Europe for its fine bricks and fireclay goods of every description, the Company's works are the largest of its kind in the world. The goods produced, for durability and other*

Opposite: Top *Bridges, Coatbridge*. Middle left *Gartsherrie Church, Coatbridge*. Bottom left *Airdrie Savings Bank, Coatbridge*. Right *Coatbridge High School*

SIXTH EDITION.

ALL COMMUNICATIONS TO BE ADDRESSED TO THE COMPANY

GLENBOIG UNION FIRE CLAY C.º L.ᵀᴰ GLENBOIG, Scotland

58 PRIZE MEDALS &   HIGHEST AWARD

DIPLOMAS OF HONOUR   WHEREVER EXHIBITED

TELEGRAPHIC ADDRESS.
"GLENBOIG. GLASGOW."
GLASGOW TELEPHONES:
NOS. 2120 AND 3009 DOUGLAS
WORKS TELEPHONE:
NO. 25 COATBRIDGE.

HEAD OFFICES
48 WEST REGENT STREET
GLASGOW

ON THE ADMIRALTY LIST
AND
CONTRACTORS TO HIS MAJESTYS
HOME & INDIAN GOVERNMENTS
AND THE
PRINCIPAL NATIONAL ARSENALS

JAMES DUNNACHIE, CHAIRMAN AND MANAGING DIRECTOR
RICHARD BAXTER, SECRETARY.

Glenboig Union Fireclay Co Ltd

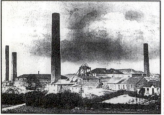

RCAHMS

Monklands District Council

Top *Certificate, Glenboig Union Fireclay Co.* Middle *Garnqueen Brickworks.* Above *Glenboig Union Fireclay Co. offices*

virtues, find no superior anywhere and its reputation stands higher than that of any other district. So much has this been the case that other manufacturers have adopted the expedient of having their letters addressed to Glenboig Post Office, thus striving to identify themselves with the name. The local clay mines also fed the nearby Garnqueen brickworks. These industrial sites have been largely cleared.

Glenboig Union Fireclay Company Offices, Main Street, 1905, James Davidson
Decorative two-storey block in yellow brickwork with contrasting red sandstone dressings and crowstepped gables, caught in mid-flight between Scots Baronial and Victorian industrial. The original acid-etched window panes retain the once famous logo of GUF. Neighbouring Garnqueen Loch forms a picturesque foreground for the extensive post-war Marnoch housing estates which rise to the north. A path here leads to the vestigial remains of **Inchnock Tower**, once the seat of the Forsythes of Dykes.

Marnoch House, Glenboig Road, *c*.1910, J M Arthur
Asymmetrical Edwardian villa, rather tucked away (now surrounded by the Marnoch housing scheme), which retains most of its original quality interiors.

New Monkland Parish launched a mission to Glenboig in 1892, then a village of over a thousand inhabitants, and two years later a new Chapel was constructed, to the design of J J Burnet (since demolished) and a missionary preacher installed. The present unremarkable Parish Church (originally the Free Church) is a little Gothic sandstone shed by George Arthur, three lancet gables to Main Street surmounted by small bellcote. **Gray's Coachworks**, once Glenboig's cinema of 1936 by Stellmacs of Glasgow, is now lamentably adapted for a non-starring role. The Caledonian Railway led south-west through Glenboig to the great grey sheds of the Gartcosh Steelworks, and its period signalbox remains at Garnqueen North Junction, red brick base supporting an external balcony, the upper glazed enclosure sheltering under generously bracketed eaves.

Glenboig Parish Church

ANNATHILL

A tiny mining village to the north of Glenboig; most of the houses originally built by William Baird & Company in three terraces to serve Bedlay Colliery and coke ovens. Bedlay produced coal for the Baird's Gartsherrie Iron Works and was one of the major employers in the Monklands, with over a thousand colliers at the height of its production. The mine closed in 1981 and the Baird terraces have been demolished, leaving this diminished outpost of a community. Even its giant pit bings have shrunk, much of the material being re-used in the construction of the neighbouring motorway.

Annathill School, **Mollinsburn Road**, 1909, J M Arthur, is a plain dominie-box, but its adjacent schoolhouse, also J M Arthur, 1902, is full of Arts & Crafts character, the five-windowed gable frontage enhanced by extravagantly overshot eaves. Half a mile further north, **North Medrox Farm** retains its big 18th-century cornmill sheltering against the hillside, once powered by water from the Spouty Braes.

Annathill Schoolhouse

MONKLAND

ANNATHILL

CLEDDANS

RIGGEND

WAT

MARNOCH

GLENBOIG

GLENMAVIS

P

WOODEND·LOCH

LOCHEND·LOCH

AIRDRIE

BARGEDDIE

COATBRIDGE

CALDERBANK

VIGILANTER

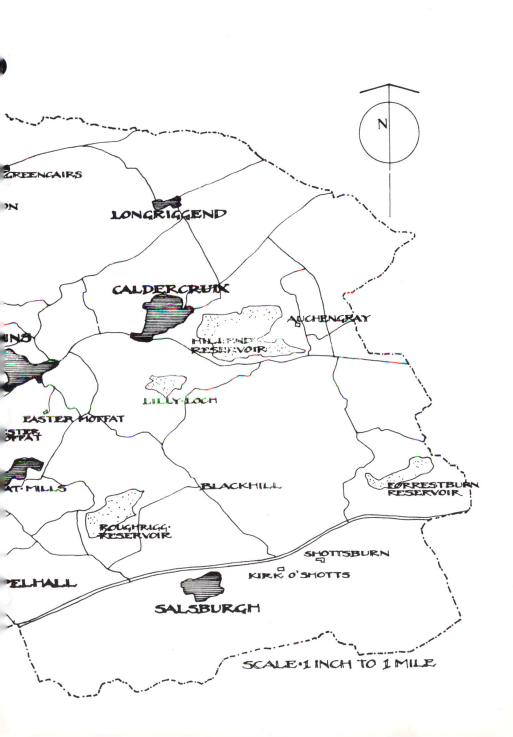

GREENCAIRS

LONGRIGGEND

CALDERCRUIX

AUCHENGRAY

HILL END
RESERVOIR

LILLY LOCH

EASTER MOFFAT

BLACKHILL

FORRESTBURN
RESERVOIR

ROUGHRIGG
RESERVOIR

SHOTTSBURN

KIRK O'SHOTTS

PELHALL

SALSBURGH

N

SCALE · 1 INCH TO 1 MILE

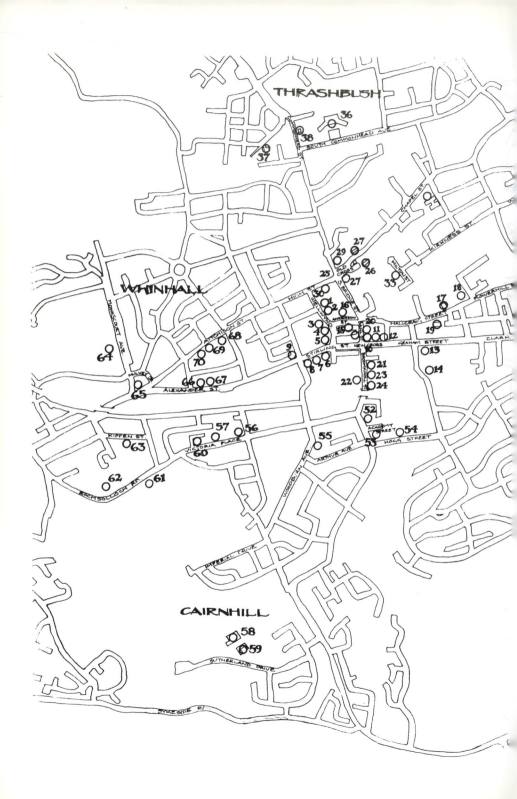

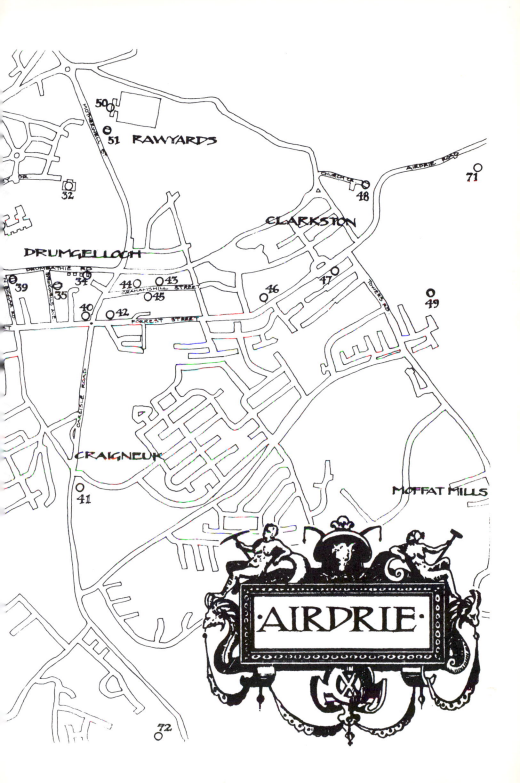

50

51 RAWYARDS

32

71

48

CLARKSTON

DRUMGELLOCH

39

34

44 43

46 47 49

35

45

40

42

FORREST STREET

CRAIGNEUK

41

MOFFAT MILLS

·AIRDRIE·

72

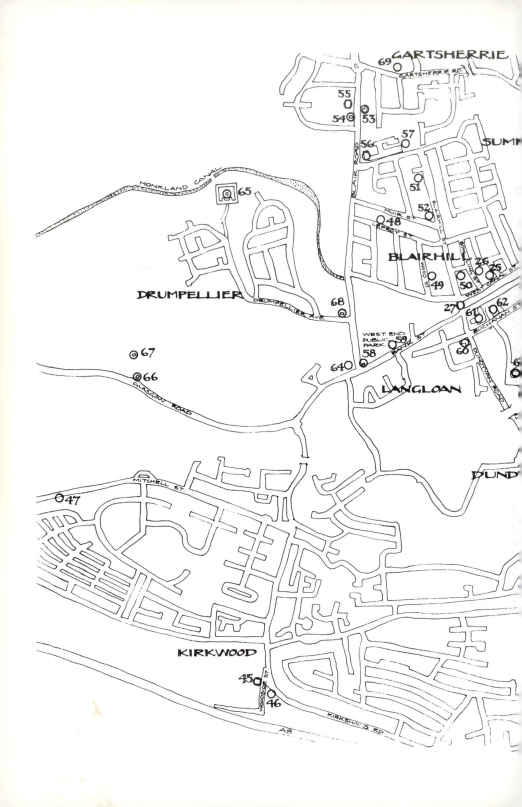

GLOSSARY

(1) Acanthus: carved leaf form
(2) Anthemion: honeysuckle-based ornament
(3) Arris: the line of a corner
(4) Apse: vaulted semicircular end to a church
(5) Architrave: a moulded frame
(6) Ashlar: squared masonry blocks, often smooth faced
(7) But and ben: two-roomed cottage
(8) Bracket: supporting piece of masonry
(9) Broken pediment: pediment with a break in the moulding
(10) Buckle quoins: decorative strapwork corner stones
(11) Bull-faced: masonry with rounded edges and face
(12) Bartizan: small projecting turret
(13) Baptistry: building for baptismal rites
(14) Bellcote: a framework for bells on a roof
(15) Campanile: bell tower
(16) Cupola: small dome on a circular base

(17) Clachan: village
(18) Crowsteps: masonry steps on a gable
(19) Corbel: a projecting block of stone
(20) Cenotaph: a monument to persons buried elsewhere
(21) Colonettes: small grouped columns
(22) Capital: the head of a column
(23) Diapered: surface decoration of continuous squares
(24) Dressings: worked masonry round openings and corners

(25) Engaged: attached (of columns)
(26) Entablature: upper part of a classical order
(27) Finial: a formal ornament at the apex of a gable
(28) Foliated: carved with leaf ornament
(29) Gushet: an angled junction of roads
(30) Jettied: the upper floors projecting, in timber construction
(31) Lancet: slender pointed arch
(32) Lantern: a small windowed turret, crowning a roof
(33) Lucarne: opening in a spire
(34) Lich-gate: covered wooden gateway with open sides
(35) Machicolation: a projecting parapet with downward openings
(36) Oculus: a round window
(37) Ogee: double curved – convex and concave
(38) Pediment: a low pitched gable over a portico
(39) Pilaster: a pier projecting slightly from a wall
(40) Plate-tracery: decorative openings with solid stone infill
    (41) Plinth: the projecting base of a wall
    (42) Quoin: dressed stone at a corner
        (43) Quatrefoil: an ornament of four-leaf shapes
        (44) Rusticated: masonry with exaggerated joints between
            blocks
      (45) Reredos: decorated screen behind an altar
      (46) Sneck: small squared stone in rubble masonry
      (47) Skewput, skewstone: supporting masonry end to a gable
          coping
      (48) Strapwork: decoration in interlaced strap forms
          (49) Swagged: ornament in garland forms
          (50) Transept: the transverse arm of a cross-plan
             church
            (51) Vitruvian scroll: classical frieze ornament in
               wave form
                (52) Wynd: lane

INDEX

ACKNOWLEDGEMENTS & BIBLIOGRAPHY

The author is grateful to all those who have assisted him in compiling this volume:

First the sponsors, Monklands District Council, in the shape of their Department of Planning & Development who provided photographs from their extensive archive; in particular to Willie Miller, who made all possible and kindly organised the scrutiny of the drafts, and Phil McWilliams for generous access to his painstaking and enthusiastic research into the architects and buildings of the area. Thanks are also due to the Department of Library Services for permission to reproduce illustrations from their local history archive, and to helpful staff at the Mitchell Library, Glasgow; the Scottish Room at Edinburgh Central Library; the local history section of Airdrie Library; the Carnegie Library in Coatbridge; as well as the Royal Commission on the Ancient and Historical Monuments of Scotland. Thanks are due also to Professor Frank Walker for access to student research on the Monklands area. Margaret Tooey deciphered much scarcely legible script and typed the final version, Helen Leng managed the production process, Charles McKean mended my poor verses and Lena Smith assisted with typing. Appreciation also to Duncan McAra for initial advice and real ale, Dr David Walker for enlightened comment on the draft, Dorothy Steedman for her high-tech publishing hardware, and Avril, Andy and Alana who were deserted while the project took shape.

The Monklands is not well served by literature about its buildings. The local history section of Airdrie Library, however, has much general material about the area.

The Official Handbooks, Airdrie Town Council, 1930 onwards; **The Official Guide to the Burgh of Airdrie**, Airdrie, 1937; **Baronial and Ecclesiastical Antiquities of Scotland**, Billings, 1845; **Report of the Trial Nelson v Baird**, Burness, 1843; **Tramways of the Monklands**, Ian Cormack, 1964; **The Official Guide to Coatbridge**, Corporation of Coatbridge, 1953 onwards; **Wm Baird & Co Ltd Coal and Ironmasters**, R D Corrins, 1974; **The Lanarkshire Miners**, Alan B Campbell, 1979; **A Century of Papermaking (1820-1920)**, Robert Craig & Sons, 1920; **Coatbridge Walks**, Peter Drummond; **Coatbridge, 3 Centuries of Change**, Drummond & Smith, 1984; **Glasgow and Lanarkshire Illustrated**, 1904; **Ordnance Gazeteer of Scotland**, Groome, 1884; **The Lives of Robert Haldane of Airthrey and James Haldane**, Alexander Haldane, 1852; **Poems, Sketches and Essays**, Janet Hamilton, 1885; **The Navvy in Scotland**, James Handley, 1970; **An Historical Sketch**, James Knox, Airdrie, 1921; **Airdrie Bards, past and present**, James Knox, 1930; **Lanarkshire Illustrated**, 1903; **The Canals of Scotland**, Lindsay; **Castellated and Domestic Architecture of Scotland Vol III**, MacGibbon & Ross, 1889; **New Monkland Parish**, McArthur, 1890; **The Rise and Progress of Coatbridge**, A Miller, 1864; **Roman Occupation of S W Scotland**, S N Miller, 1952; **The Monkland Tradition**, T Miller, 1958; **The Crannog at Lochend**, Coatbridge, Glasgow Archaeological Society, James Monteith 1932; **The Scottish Handloom Weavers (1790-1850)**, Norman Murray, 1978; **Origins of the Scottish Railway System (1772-1844)**, C J A Robertson, 1983; **Statistical Accounts of Scotland**, 1799, 1845; **Monkland and Kirkintilloch Railway**, Strathkelvin District Libraries and Museums, 1971; **A Stone Age Site at Woodend Loch**, Society of Antiquities of Scotland, 1949; **Stewart & Lloyd (1903-1953)**, Stewart & Lloyd Ltd, 1953; **The Monkland Canal, a Sketch of the early History**, George Thomson, 1945; **Airdrie, a Brief Historical Sketch**, Thomson, 1972; **Drumpellier Cricket Club (1850-1906)**, John Thomson, 1908; **The Growth of the Monklands**, Thomson, 1947; **Journals regarding the Monkland Canal (1770-1773)**, James Watt.

The RIAS Bookshops

Located in the centres of Edinburgh and Glasgow, the RIAS
Bookshops are the largest specialist architecture and building
bookshops in Scotland. There is a wide range of legal and technical
books in addition to volumes on design, including many beautiful
coffee table books. Both RIAS Bookshops now sell and accept Book
Tokens. Bookbank has been installed in our Edinburgh shop - we
are able to research and order all British books in print.

OTHER RIAS PUBLICATIONS

THE SCOTTISH THIRTIES *"McKean is never boring, far-fetched on
occasions, perhaps, but essentially on the side of the angels, balancing visual
acuity with perceptive, often witty comment. There are more than 400
black and white photographs, in addition to colour photographs and
drawings in this handsome volume"* THE SCOTSMAN

AUTHOR, CHARLES McKEAN. ISBN 0 7073 0494 6 **£8.50**

THE ARCHITECTURE OF THE SCOTTISH RENAISSANCE
*"... the European Renaissance had a profound and exciting impact on
Scottish culture - an impact that was expressed forcefully in the architecture
of the period"* THE SCOTSMAN

EDITOR, DR DEBORAH HOWARD. PAPERBACK **£2.00**

TAKE A LETTER *"... which I have thoroughly enjoyed and shall pass on to
my daughter, who is a youthful practising architect with much to learn
about real life"*

AUTHOR, SINCLAIR GAULDIE. PAPERBACK ISBN 1873190 00 X **£5.00**

WINNERS & LOSERS *"...should illustrate the fascinating, and
frequently controversial, course of architectural competitions in Scotland
since Craig's plan for the New Town of Edinburgh in 1766"*

AUTHOR, ROGER EMMERSON. PAPERBACK ISBN 1 873190 03 4 **£2.95**

These RIAS books: and books on Scottish Architecture are all
available from the RIAS Bookshop,
15 Rutland Square, Edinburgh EH1 2BE
031-229 7545

and
545 Sauchiehall St, Glasgow G3 7PQ
041-221 6496

ARCHITECTURAL
——— GUIDES ———
TO SCOTLAND

The acclaimed RIAS/Landmark Trust series of
Architectural Guides to Scotland is essential reading for
people interested in the built history of the country.

SERIES EDITOR: CHARLES McKEAN

Already Published

EDINBURGH: by Charles McKean.

DUNDEE: by Charles McKean and David Walker.

STIRLING AND THE TROSSACHS: by Charles McKean 1985.

ABERDEEN: by W A Brogden 1986. Now in its 2nd edition.

THE SOUTH CLYDE ESTUARY: by Frank Arneil Walker 1986.

CLACKMANNAN AND THE OCHILS: by Adam Swan 1987.

THE DISTRICT OF MORAY: by Charles McKean 1987.

CENTRAL GLASGOW: by Charles McKean, David Walker,
Frank Arneil Walker 1989.

BANFF & BUCHAN: by Charles McKean 1990.

SHETLAND: by Mike Finnie 1990.

FIFE: by Glen Pride 1991.

ORKNEY: by Leslie Burgher 1991.

ROSS & CROMARTY: by Elizabeth Beaton 1992.

Forthcoming

NORTH CLYDE ESTUARY: CENTRAL LOWLANDS:
AYRSHIRE & ARRAN: BORDERS & BERWICK

The series is winner of the
Glenfiddich Living Scotland Award 1985.